Praise for the author and

"The roadmap laid out in *The Power of People Skills* set our business up to quintuple in sales. We've learned how to fix ongoing personnel issues once and for all, attract top talent, and spend our time focused on results, not on internal staffing problems. I highly recommend it to you—it's worked for us."

—John de Jonge, owner and CEO, Artex Barn Solutions

"'Your staff is so friendly and seem to love their work! How did you find so many great people?' are questions we are frequently asked. The answer, quite simply, is Trevor Throness and the tools he teaches about in *The Power of People Skills*. It was Trevor who patiently guided us through the process of assembling, then mentoring, a star team. He also taught us the essentials of creating an enjoyable and productive work environment—for owners, managers, and staff. *The Power of People Skills* is a must-read, how-to guide for people dealing with people."

—Charlotte Lepp, co-founder Lepp Farm Market

"If you're interested in permanently solving your chronic people problems, this book is for you. We used to spend a lot of time dealing with these issues, but after implementing Trevor's tools, we now spend 90 percent of our time making our product better and acquiring new customers. Sales and profits are way up, and we're all having fun again."

—Ted Visscher, CEO, Visscher Specialty Products

"Choosing to work with Trevor and using the tools described in this book has been one of the best investments of time and money that we have made at Frontline. The results have been outstanding, as the company experienced consecutive years of 50%+ revenue growth while sustaining a healthy margin and improving team unity, focus and purpose."

—Justin Mitchell, president and managing partner,
Frontline Real Estate

"*The Power of People Skills* shines a light on the number one issue in every company. People. I personally have benefitted from the skills Trevor has outlined, and would recommend you put it to the top of your pile."

—Clayton White, CEO and managing partner,
Alliance Concrete Pumps

"Trevor's tools helped us move from the middle of the pack to being selected by the *Financial Post* as one of the top 25 charities in the country (out of 86,000). I highly recommend his new book to you."
—Bernie Willock, CEO, FH Canada

"Trevor's strategic and aggressive focus in the area of people and company alignment has helped our extremely fast-growth business become what it is today. I've experienced Trevor's approach first hand, and it's been crucial to sustain our growth. I can't imagine a business that wouldn't benefit greatly from the lessons outlined in this perceptive book."
—Brian Antenbring, founder and CEO,
TEEMA Solutions Group Inc.

"In his new book, Trevor teaches the skills, tools, and insights needed to meet their people challenges. Trevor's HR strategies have set us up to grow double digits consistently for 10 years and running. His insights in how people work, and the skills and strategies needed to build the most engaged work force possible, are tremendous."
—Dave Van Belle, CEO, Van Belle Nurseries

"Using the tools laid out in the book, I went from seriously considering selling everything, to acquiring seven additional stores, while reducing my time operating them by 90 percent. This gave me my life back and allowed me time to pursue new ventures. To say the process works is an understatement."
—Derrick Westbrook, Booster Juice multi-store franchisee,
Meat and Bread/Noodle Box restaurant chain partner

"We decided to use Trevor's methodology in our full-service law firm. At first, we resisted, telling him, 'This just won't work with a law firm.' But we persisted, and the results have been remarkable: our client base and profits have steadily improved, and staff engagement and morale is the healthiest that it's ever been."
—Doug Lester Q.C., managing partner, RDM Law

THE POWER OF PEOPLE SKILLS

HOW TO ELIMINATE 90% OF YOUR
HR PROBLEMS AND DRAMATICALLY
INCREASE TEAM AND COMPANY
MORALE AND PERFORMANCE

TREVOR THRONESS

CAREER
PRESS

Wayne, N.J.

THE POWER OF PEOPLE SKILLS
EDITED BY JODI BRANDON
TYPESET BY KRISTIN GOBLE
Cover design by Howard Grossman/12e Design
People image by Rawpixel.com/shutterstock
Printed in the U.S.A.

To order this title, please call toll-free 1-800-CAREER-1 (NJ and Canada: 201-848-0310) to order using VISA or MasterCard, or for further information on books from Career Press.

CAREER
PRESS

The Career Press, Inc.
12 Parish Drive
Wayne, NJ 07470
www.careerpress.com

Library of Congress Cataloging-in-Publication Data

CIP Data Available Upon Request.

To my parents, Harald and Edna Throness,
who modeled true leadership
by pouring out their lives serving others.

ACKNOWLEDGMENTS

Thanks to my many clients for allowing me to field test these ideas in the real world. Thanks to Dave Van Belle for helping to develop the Coach and Connect tool, which we tested in his business before using it in other businesses and industries. Thanks to Gazelles International for introducing me to the concept of assessing people according to quadrants. Thanks to Jim Collins for the idea of using core values in a business (Built to Last). Thanks to my beautiful wife, Jenn, for her encouragement and editing of early drafts of the book. If only we weren't married so that we could have a torrid affair. Thanks to Julia (who helped with editing), Sam, Ella, and Will, our kids, who have provided so much laughter, meaning, and growth over the past 20 years. Thank you to my brothers Laurie (for lots of editing help) and Lyndon (for drawing the illustrations) and to Doug Lester for critiquing the manuscript with a lawyer's eye for detail, helping me avoid embarrassing mistakes.

And thanks to John Coltrane, Stan Getz, Dave Brubeck, Miles Davis, Oscar Peterson, Charlie Parker, Thelonious Monk, the whole Marsalis family, Sonny

Rollins, Frank, Ella, Mel, and many other jazz greats for keeping me company during the hours spent in my office writing this manuscript.

CONTENTS

INTRODUCTION

I grew up in a leadership family. My dad was the pastor of what was then the largest church in Canada. At the same time, he founded a charter school that now has 1,200 students attending. My mom had a huge heart and ran programs for large numbers of mentally challenged individuals. Her greatest tribute was to be regularly visited by a man with Down syndrome, who rode his bike across town to see her while she was on her deathbed. Like the vast majority of church leaders the world over, they made little money, served wholeheartedly, and entertained no hint of scandal.

In their spare time (!) my parents planted churches in towns around ours, and that's where my siblings and I came in. We were expected to be leaders. So from an early age, I taught classes of kids, worked as a camp counselor and a youth group leader, and (to my great chagrin) even stepped up with a musical selection from time to time. My earliest memories focus on working with and for people.

After college (where I worked as a resident director and as a leader in many volunteer roles), I started my career as a youth pastor, working with teenagers, volunteer staff, and parents in a very fast-growing church. In an effort to cope with all of the issues attendant to growth, we spent a lot of time touring the world, interviewing and learning from the best leaders and motivators of volunteers on the planet. These are exceptionally gifted people. It's one thing to lead people who are paid to follow you, and quite another to lead volunteers who don't receive a paycheck from you and could just as easily stay at home.

I learned from many of the key leaders in the church world at that time. In Seoul, Korea, I toured the largest church in the world (Yoido Full Gospel Church, then at about 700,000 members), and later had an opportunity to speak with the lead pastor, who gave leadership to more than 500 pastors and tens of thousands of volunteers. This was a mind-expanding learning experience for me, as I spent the majority of my work time recruiting volunteer leaders, and devising new strategies to train, engage, and deploy them.

Then I moved into the business world, working for a mid-market company that operated on a global scale. There, I was amazed to find that leadership didn't spend much time (or even any time at all) on issues like employee engagement, organizational health, and attracting and retaining star people.

The practice then was to run ads and hire people to fill a spot, and then forget about them until they quit or caused trouble that required intervention by management. I was shocked. I always assumed that the business world had this issue dialed, but I found to my amazement that this non-strategy around people was pretty much normal; we weren't unique. Our suppliers and customers ran their businesses in pretty much the same way. To me, this seemed like madness, a tremendous waste of money and talent. In my previous life, I had seen what engaged, trained people were capable of doing.

After spending seven years in the trenches putting some of my employee engagement ideas into practice, I realized that my true passion was to work with business leaders to find ways to win on the "people" side of the business. In 2003, I went out on my own and have never looked back. I care deeply about these issues.

Today, I help leaders navigate the challenges associated with growth, and most of these challenges are rooted in people issues. As complicated as they seem, these issues can be fixed. Imagine: no more working with people who you wouldn't rehire if you could do it all over again. No more going home to talk over people issues with your spouse. No more stressing out during the day, wondering if delegated jobs are getting done right. In short, no more grappling with chronic, nagging people issues.

I've worked in many businesses across multiple industries in which, when we're done, the business has every key seat filled with true A-level players, or "stars." A star is simply someone who "gets it." Stars share the attitudes that are important to you, and are committed to getting a lot done. A star is typically three times more productive than an "okay" person.

A non-star in a key seat costs the business between two and 15 times their annual salary, depending on the role. Do the math: Fixing this problem is paramount. Learning to assemble and deploy a team comprised of the right players is the most important skill you can develop in business.

There's a lot of talk and ink poured out today about how to build a great culture, but I believe that it isn't a complicated equation. Simply put:

A great culture insists that every person on the team play as a star.

A poor culture tolerates chronic underperformance.

I help implement tools that enhance communication, and focus and engage employees. We live in a new era in which employees aren't content to show up and shut off their brains. Putting all of your effort into coaching the right people, and getting them singing from the same song sheet, saves you money and makes you money too. This book gives you the road map to permanently solve your people problems.

I already know something about you, too: if you're reading this book, you're trying to figure out how to get better at handling people issues. I've written this book for:

- **Business owners and managers.** If you're the onsite manager of either the mother ship or a branch office, getting the people part of the business right is your biggest challenge and the biggest indicator of whether you'll succeed or fail.
- **Regional managers working with multi-site businesses.** If you're on the road working with

several business units—whether the units are corporately owned or part of a franchise—this book is for you. You must be able to advise and coach your managers on how to handle their biggest stress: how to handle their people issues.

- **Young leaders being asked to step up into a new role.** The thing that will make or break you in your new role is your ability to win the confidence of your players and then see each of them achieve their potential. Far and away, the most important skill for you to develop is the ability to attract, retain, and develop star players.

- **Board members.** If you've been asked to sit on the board of any organization, the main issue that you'll have in front of you is people. This book is written to educate you on how to get much, much better at the skill of evaluating and working with them.

- **Not-for-profit leaders.** Whether you're leading an NGO, a government office, a church, or an academic institution, many of your issues are the same as those of every business. Whenever you get a group of people together trying to accomplish something, you run into the same set of challenges. You're not immune just because you're trying to change the world.

A Word About the Format

To save you time, each chapter ends with a chapter summary and *people action steps* that you can immediately implement.

Though the case studies and stories are true, names and identifying details have been changed.

1

Attracting Stars Is Lucrative— and So Much More

"If I were running a company today, I would have one priority above all others: to acquire as many of the best people as I could. I'd put off everything else to fill my bus. Because things are going to come back. My flywheel is going to start to turn. And the single biggest constraint on the success of my organization is the ability to get and to hang on to enough of the right people."

—Jim Collins, American business consultant
and author of *Good to Great: Why Some
Companies Make the Leap...and Others Don't*

Businesses that have "A" players in every key seat outperform businesses that don't by between three and ten times, depending on which source you read. Compared to getting this right, nothing else in your business matters much; it's the issue that should be uppermost in your mind, and, like a coach of a sports team, you should be spending at least half of your head space planning, plotting, and scheming over how you're going to achieve this goal.

If you don't believe it, think for a minute about your very best employee. What would you do without that person? How would you feel if he left the company? How many people would it take to replace him? Now imagine what your business would look like if you had someone as good as him in every important role in your business. Forget your business—what would your *life* look like? "A" players are a joy to work with!

If you're taking an issue home with you; if you're talking over a business problem with your spouse; if you're lying awake at night, mulling things over in your mind; if you're "stuck" while facing an impossible hurdle; if you feel burned out or you're thinking of selling the business and doing something easier, the vast majority of the time you're wrestling with a people problem.

That problem may *appear* to be a financial or inventory or logistics or customer service issue, but usually the presenting issue is just the dummy light blinking on the dashboard. In other words, the "issue" is only a symptom that can be traced back to a root cause, and usually that root cause is a person. It might be a great person in the wrong seat; it might be an awful person in an important seat; it might be someone who was once great and who is now sitting in a seat that has outgrown him or her.

Incidentally, leaders don't usually burn out due to overwork, because productive work that you're good at can be very energizing. More often, burnout comes from playing with weak players. This forces you, the leader, to sit in your own seat, *plus* cover other, weaker players' positions (which are often ones that you're not good at or interested in doing). Being forced to do things that you're not great at is exhausting.

As a Leader, You're in the People Business

Once you have employed more than five people, you're no longer in the food service/manufacturing/retail business, you're in the people business! Although you can use many great initiatives and programs to upgrade your company, this one—the people business—must precede them all; if it doesn't, you're throwing your money away. Without the right people in the right seats, having the right strategy doesn't really matter—nor does having a war chest of cash or a great business idea, or a host of employee training sessions, or the latest, greatest quality program. Without the right people in the right seats, nothing works. Best team wins!

If you want to change your life, reduce your stress, and make your business lucrative and fun, first you're going to have to sort out your people problems.

The Container Store is very public about its winning equation: one great person = three good people. When founders Kip Tindell and Garrett Boone opened their first store in 1978, their organizing principle in human resources was simply to persuade their best, most loyal customers to join the company, become top-performing employees, and pay them more—a lot more—than the industry average. The founders also invested a tremendous amount into them, giving first-year full-time employees 263 hours of formal training (compared to the retail industry average of eight).[1]

In a sector in which the average employee doesn't even stay a year, turnover at the Container Store is less than 10 percent, and a third of the company's 2,500 workers come from referrals. The company reported 20 percent growth every year since inception to 2014. In short, the Container Store focuses on finding top players—or what we will refer to from here on as "stars"—and their superior results follow.

Attracting and retaining stars is clearly lucrative for a company, but it is also so much more. Stars don't need to be motivated. They need to be coached, trained, career counseled, encouraged, and sometimes corrected or even disciplined, but never motivated. They're self-motivated. They make fewer mistakes, have better relationships with customers, and are never at the center of internal drama. Because you and others trust them, everything moves faster. They aren't involved in efficiency-killing turf wars. They don't need someone to double-check their work or repair their relationship problems.

Finding people that you both trust and love is not just about generating warm feelings, either. These people show up on the bottom line of your income statement.

In *Good to Great*, Jim Collins's ground-breaking study of good companies that became great (companies that beat their closest competitor by three or more times over a fifteen-year period), the first two steps every great company took was to, first, get the right leader and, second, "get the right people on the bus, and the wrong people off the bus."[2]

Your Top Three Priorities as a Leader

Your job isn't easy, but it's not complicated, either. It's simply to:

1. Find the best possible players for your team.
2. Tell them clearly what they need to do in order to win in their role.
3. Let them know how they're doing and coach them on a regular basis.

These three tasks represent the main themes of the chapters that follow. They aren't complex; in fact, on the face of it, they seem ridiculously simple. But have you ever worked for a company that followed these three rules? If you're like most people, it's not likely. Most leaders are content to work with sub-par players, assume they'll figure the job out on their own, and never get around to giving them feedback unless something has gone outrageously wrong.

But I believe in finding the best players, making sure they are clear on what they are there to do, and then using every engagement with them as an opportunity to train, model, coach, and build their self-confidence.

As a young guy in a sales role, I was challenged by a speaker on tape to write out my one-phrase job description. This interesting exercise cuts through a lot of clutter. Mine was "to increase hot tub sales through existing and new retailers." That's it. This obvious revelation was tremendously focusing for me. I taped it to my computer monitor. It reminded me that I wasn't there to answer phones or compose emails or attend meetings or talk with guys in the factory, although I did all those things. My job was to sell.

When that kind of clarity is paired with regular feedback and coaching, results will follow.

Learning to Lead Your Team Well

Market research firm Harris Interactive surveyed more than 23,000 people employed full-time in industries including accommodation/food services, automotive, banking/finance, communications, education, healthcare, military, public administration/government, retail, technology services, and telecommunications. The poll was designed to measure "the execution gap"—that is, the gap between an organization setting a goal and actually achieving it. Here are some of their shocking findings:

- Only 37 percent of respondents knew the company's goals.
- Only 20 percent were enthusiastic about those goals.
- Only 20 percent could see how they could support those goals.
- Only 15 percent felt empowered to work toward those goals.
- Only 20 percent fully trusted the company they worked for.[3]

Imagine if this were your team. Less than half of your staff would know exactly what they were supposed to be doing. One in five would be excited about their job. One in five would be sure about what they were supposed to be doing at work, and in any case, fewer than one in five would feel trusted enough to work toward the goals that they didn't understand in the first place. And the really painful kicker is that one in five wouldn't even trust the leadership team enough to care if they won or if they lost to the competition.

How would you feel about being on a team like that? How would you feel if you were the coach of a team like that? Are you sure that you're not?

If you want to build an amazing team, it may require a shift in thinking about your own role. We often use the term *manager* to describe someone who is in charge of people. However, this term reinforces the illusion that people can, in fact, be "managed." We need to begin to think of ourselves as *leaders* or, better yet, *coaches*.

A manager builds, streamlines, and monitors systems and processes. A manager works with things, because things—such as inventory levels, food and labor costs, allocation of capital, or product quality—can be managed. You can manage things, but people are inherently unmanageable. They are filled with unruly emotions and personal problems, and, even though they may have the skills you need, can display an amazing range and variety of attitudes. People require leaders.

Most weak "people managers" view the people side of their role as a noose around their neck that they would love to be able to slide out of. They don't realize that "who" questions are always more important than "what" questions. In truth, you can't be a people manager. You can only be a poor leader who leads people badly, or a good one who leads people well.

You've gotten this far, so it's clear which one you want to be, so let's get started on the journey.

People Action Steps

- Find the best possible players for your team.
- Tell them clearly what they need to do in order to win in their role.
- Let them know how they're doing and coach them on a regular basis.

In Summary

- If you can build a team of "stars" all rowing in the same direction, you can dominate any industry.
- Companies that do the hard work of finding star players for every key seat are much more profitable than those that don't. It's the first and most important step on the path to achieving results up to three times those of your closest competitor.
- Learning to hire and retain stars is the key to winning in your business.
- You can't manage people. You can only lead them well or badly.

2

Determine Whether You Have Stars (or Not)

"I like Tom. He doesn't do a lot of work around here. He shows zero initiative. He's not a team player. He's never wanted to go that extra mile. Tom is exactly what I'm looking for in a government employee."

—Ron Swanson, fictional character
in *Parks and Recreation*

Like every school in North America at the time, my junior high school had a simple method of determining who played for the school sports teams and who didn't. We formed teams in phys ed class; went out to the baseball diamond, basketball court, hockey rink, or volleyball court; and tried our hand at playing the various games. The most talented kids couldn't help but see that they were gifted in their sport and worked their hardest to be the best of the best in the school. These kids became the backbone of the school's competitive teams.

Among the kids with average levels of talent, some were motivated to try out for the school teams and work their hardest to get better and raise their level of play. Others belonging to the middle pack were content to play at an intramural level, just for the fun of the sport.

Then there were the 10 percent of kids who made the top 90 percent possible: the truly terrible athletes. I have good intel on this group, as I served as their poster boy throughout my school years. Membership requirements of this group included (but were not limited to):

- Proudly wearing a yellow "participant" ribbon, given to everyone with any level of brain function who decided to show up at the annual track meet.
- Being hit in the head with various balls due to distractions (such as watching clouds or fantasizing about which superhero would have the best chance of overpowering Superman [answer: none]).
- Enduring the leaden stares of team members when we were assigned to their team in gym class.

Ultimately, the job of members of this group was to sit in the stands and cheer—and find something else to do that we were good at.

Today, this method is viewed as cruel by the crowd that awards a "winner" ribbon to everyone—whether the participant came in first or 10th—but I disagree. Not being a winner in sports actually helped me to focus on what I was great at and had passion for, and that was music. I saved my money to see many (now-dead) jazz greats in concert, competed at a regional and national level, and acquired a skill that's still a joy to me.

We're all good at different things. If a person isn't the right fit in his current role, that's likely a sign that there is a job he will be great at—somewhere else.

For a variety of reasons, if you're like most leaders, you tend to grade your people higher than they really are. It may be because you're afraid to see them hurt because they're such nice people, or that you see *yourself* as a nice person who wouldn't dream of causing pain to another. Maybe it's because assigning a lower grade would force you to have some hard, maybe unpleasant, conversations resulting in you not being liked anymore.

We'll deal head-on with some of these fears in Chapter 4, but for now, suffice it to say that not being honest with yourself about the performance of each of your team members doesn't help you, doesn't help them, and ensures that the performance of the whole team will suffer.

The 4 Essential Questions

Let's try completing a simple, honest assessment of each of your key people. Write down the names of these main players, and ask yourself the following four questions about each one.

1. If you could do it all over again, would you rehire her?
2. Does he take your stress away?

3. How would you feel if she quit?
4. What if everyone in your business was just like him?

1. If You Could Do It All Over Again, Would You Rehire Her?

Knowing what you know now, if you could go back in time to when you made your initial hiring decision, would you rehire her and be excited to do so? In this thought experiment, you get to do a complete do-over. There are no consequences to deal with. You don't have to review the history of why you made the decision you did at the time. You don't have to think through questions of replacing the person or face the prospect of potentially painful conversations in the future. Just cut through the clutter and answer the question: would you rehire if you could do it over?

The mark of a star is that you answer with a resounding YES! to this question every time.

2. Does He Take Your Stress Away?

With that person in the role, does your stress evaporate? Do you go home relaxed in the knowledge that everything's covered now that he's on the job, or do you worry about what he's doing? Do you double-check his work before it goes out? Do you create systems for him so his mistakes will be caught (by you or someone else)?

You know that you're carrying someone else's stress when you go home and think about issues *he* should be thinking about. The reason you hired him in the first place, and continue to pay him now, is so he will do his job and you won't have to think about it anymore. Why should you pay someone to do a job and still carry part of the load and stress of that job? It just doesn't make sense.

Have you been accused of being a poor delegator? Maybe the issue isn't your skill in delegation, but the calibre of person you are choosing. I find that even natural micro-managers find it much easier to let go when they're relinquishing an important task to someone who has shown a history of caring about the job as much as they do and of getting results. A reluctance to delegate often reflects on your experience: you've been burned in the past by delegating to the wrong person.

When a star is in charge, you relax; you're confident that he will take care of it.

3. How Would You Feel if She Quit?

Would you feel delighted, relieved, ambivalent, or devastated?

When a weak performer leaves a company, she often fantasizes about how no one will be able to get along without her. She pictures the faces of her crestfallen customers who hear the news of her departure. She smirks with satisfaction as she envisions former colleagues awash with work they didn't even know existed and have no idea how to complete. She believes that soon people throughout the organization will realize with dismay how wrong they were not to appreciate her indispensable contribution to the company.

What she doesn't know is that usually these people are dancing with delight at her departure. Rather than dismay, colleagues feel a tremendous sense of relief and even of joy after a low performer leaves. Customers and coworkers are only too happy not to have to deal with the behaviours that made her an underperformer in the first place. There's certainly no sorrow on display.

On the other hand, when a star leaves, her leaders and coworkers feel devastated—maybe even sick. They may go into a funk, wondering how they'll go on without her. They regain equilibrium in time, but there are no feelings of ambivalence about her departure, and certainly no relief or delight.

Many times I've received a call at an odd hour from a CEO who has just found out that a key star player is leaving. Often the CEO is stunned. There may be long silences on the phone as he slowly absorbs the multi-faceted consequences he will have to face due to losing his star.

One of the hallmarks of a star is that no one wants her to leave.

4. What if Everyone in Your Business Was Just Like Him?

Does he bring the average up or down?

If everyone on the team played at his level, would the team be upgraded or downgraded? A below-average player will obviously bring down the performance of the entire team.

As a teenager, I had a summer job that involved erecting metal Quonset huts on farmers' yards throughout small towns in Alberta. These huts were made up of semi-circular bands of corrugated steel secured together with thousands, maybe millions, of bolts. My job was to wait for my partner on the outside of the Quonset hut to insert a bolt into the pre-drilled hole of the galvanized steel band, thread a nut onto the bolt, and then hold it in place with a wrench while he tightened it with an air-powered drill. We performed this maneuver thousands of times each day. My partner and I didn't find this career very rewarding, and we weren't very good at it, either. We regularly fumbled with and dropped the nuts and bolts, and made endless trips up and down ladders to retrieve them. We were not the superstars of the Quonset hut–building crew.

As the days wore on, however, one of the two-man teams grew so efficient at this operation that they would beat the rest of us by two, or even three, times. They raced up and down the ladders, firing bolts into the steel bands with military precision and zeal. They were positive and eager, and seemed to love the work. Their passion was a complete mystery to me at the time. This summer job was defined by a bare-bones existence: eating every meal at the jobsite, sleeping on garage floors by night, and tightening thousands of bolts by day. This didn't precisely match my self-image as an urban sophisticate. But looking back on it now, I wonder what the boss thought about my two-man team, what the stars thought about the non-stars, or how many Quonset huts the entire crew could have built if we all shared the same skills and drive as those top performers.

If everyone on your team is a star, your business will rock and your life will be bliss. So why aren't you bending *all* your focus and effort to attract and keep the stars?

Separating the Great From the Not-as-Great

As we've seen, building a great team is the most important job of the leader. Here's what great looks like compared to not-as-great:

Great Employees	Not-as-Great Employees
Are punctual	"Try" to be on time
Get involved	Issue orders and expect people to obey
Make great hires and fix bad hires when hiring mistakes are made	Build weak teams of non-stars
Are honest	Cut corners and push integrity boundaries
Look for challenge/opportunity	Look for a job
Work with passion	Lack drive and do the "same old, same old"
Learn from their mistakes	Make lots of mistakes and don't learn much

Stay until the job is done	Make excuses and delegate back to you
Steadily improve their skillset	Plateau and stay there
Regularly hit their targets	Are "almost there" on a regular basis
Work well with others	Stir up drama; engage in turf wars
Focus on solutions	Explain why things can't be done
Figure out tough situations	Face challenges, make excuses, and give up

And here's the real kicker: Ironically, stars often earn nearly the same as non-stars. This is true in any profession. When you choose a family physician, consider that 50 percent of all physicians graduated in the bottom half of their class. (Assuming that 100 percent of medical students have graduated from a given class, it follows that 50 percent of them would have had to be in the bottom half of the class, right?) They all charge the same amount of money for their services, but they're not all created equal. This is also true of lawyers, purchasers, CEOs, electricians, mechanics, operations managers, barbers, sales managers, and retail clerks. Some are amazing at what they do, and some aren't. And they usually earn about the same amount of money.

This established, why not make a commitment—right now—to attract the very best employees for your company? It probably won't cost you more!

The 10 Sure Signs of a Star

Regardless of salary or role, the stars on your team are bound to have some things in common:

1. Maturity.
2. Passion.
3. Drive.
4. Integrity.
5. Reliability.
6. Positivity.
7. Run with a star crowd.
8. Bloom where they've been planted.
9. Track record of success.
10. Respected by colleagues.

1. Maturity

Maturity is the ability to see things from someone else's perspective. A mature person is a joy to be around. He doesn't bring drama to the workplace. He can be objective about his areas of strength. He owns his mistakes. And he can see things not just from his perspective, but from the perspective of other people as well.

Immature people see problems from their perspective only, and often have strong opinions about anyone who doesn't bring immediate benefit to them. In their minds, people who come into conflict with them become "bad" people, and they are quick to pass on their judgments to others. How a person sees the world tells you a great deal about them.

As a young salesman, I dealt with a customer who was a very difficult person. When a phone call came in from him, my heart sank and I steeled myself to the unpleasant task of talking with him for the next 10 or 15 minutes.

He owned a business, and had a very low opinion of everyone around him. His wife (and both during and after his marriage, his girlfriend) was not up to the job of pleasing him as he deserved. Everyone who he did business with (including me) was constantly trying to cheat him. Worst of all, in his mind, were his employees, some of whom were family members. According to him, they were forever trying to steal time, product, and cash. He was a huge energy drain and tiresome to be around.

After one of his anti-employee rants, I finally asked, "Do you realize that you're describing precisely how I feel about *you?* You, too, are forever trying to get every last nickel out of us [as his supplier] by faking quality issues, submitting bogus warranty claims, and demanding free product and free use of our technician's time. So, believe me, I know exactly how you feel. Could it be that you're training your employees to act like you do?" He surprised me by laughing nervously, looking at his shoes, walking away, and being more circumspect with how he spoke to me after that.

As Ralph Waldo Emerson once said, "People seem not to see that their opinion of the world is also a confession of their character."

2. Passion

All stars have passion for what they do. They care about their customers, and they care about the company. Passion doesn't necessarily look the same for everyone. Some people are demonstrative and enthusiastic, whereas others are quiet and determined. But for stars, the passion shines through over time.

Some people excel in high-profile positions. The spotlight naturally gravitates to them; they get lots of attention, and that's fine. But often there are quiet, unassuming stars if you take the time to look.

I once worked with a multi-national company that nominated, and then selected by vote, its Most Valuable Player of the Year. Each year the award went to one of the top brass, or to an outstanding salesperson who was well-known and had "star power."

One year they were brainstorming about nominees, and, out of the blue, Jackie's name was thrown into the discussion. Jackie was a bookkeeper who had been with the company for...nobody really knew how long. She was part of the woodwork. Furthermore, she had an outstanding attitude, was uplifting to her colleagues, and did her job faithfully, well, and without complaint. She was considerate to the people around her, showing practical displays of kindness and love. She was positive and polite, and cared deeply about the company.

Jackie was also timid as a mouse and hardly said a word. Though she was a force for good on the team, unquestionably lifting the average, she didn't spend a lot of time with her colleagues. She ate her lunch at her desk and went home directly after work, avoiding situations that might draw attention to herself. She was nothing like the well-known, star-power people who had won in the past. Yet Jackie was recognized as being a true star by her coworkers, who chose her in a landslide after she was nominated by the executive team.

People in any role can be stars, and passion looks different for different people.

3. Drive

Stars care about seeing things completed. They don't give up, but push to see the job done well. They don't need you to kick-start them. They can do that on their own. They need your advice and encouragement and mentorship, but not your motivation; that's intrinsic to who they are.

If you find yourself thinking up schemes to motivate a person to do the basic jobs that he is already paid to do, something is amiss. Bonuses should be paid for behavior that's above and beyond what the basic job requires. A wage isn't a "showing up bonus" that must then be supplemented to get day-to-day work done.

4. Integrity

Although every star wants to win, a true star knows where the boundaries are. He doesn't cut corners with customers.

He doesn't do shady side deals. He doesn't quietly take product home for his own use. You never wonder if he can be trusted with important information or even with cash. He has integrity.

I've seen strong performers passed over for promotion for simple things that they might not have noticed or thought about, like stealing time from the company by taking breaks that were too long or taking home left-over "defective" product. Integrity matters.

I once worked for a company that employed a top-tier salesperson. He was very good at moving product, and was beloved by his customers and (grudgingly) admired by his colleagues. He outsold them all by a wide margin. However, if his customers had known how he spoke about them when they weren't there, they may not have been quite as thrilled with his behavior.

Inside the office he would regale his small circle of young hero-worshippers with tales of how he had duped customers and prospects into deals that were great for him and for the company, but were not ideal for them in the long run. He would tell "white lies" to customers on the phone about missed delivery dates or reasons for quality issues.

Though he was viewed as a valuable player, he wasn't trusted or respected, and when management considered people to promote, he was quickly eliminated from the list despite being talented, smart, and driven.

5. Reliability

A star is someone who can be counted on to do what she says she'd do. You don't wonder if your star is going to forget to wake up and open the store in the morning when it's her responsibility. You don't wake up with a start in the middle of the night wondering if she remembered to make that important call. She is reliable; if she said she will do it, she'll get it done.

Her reliability takes your stress away. It's pretty tough to live with someone whom you can't count on.

6. Positivity

Stars all have positive attitudes. I'm not talking about whether they're cheerful in the morning (they may be), but about whether or not they have an attitude that says, "We'll solve this." They look for solutions and move every situation forward in a positive way. I've conducted many hiring interviews, and throughout a process that is quite involved and takes a fair amount of time, I'm always looking for this one quality above all others.

Non-stars come up against obstacles and shrink back from them. They have all sorts of reasons for doing so, but at the end of the day their tummy hurts and they have to go home. Stars encounter walls and figure out ways to climb, dig under, go around, or blast though them.

Positivity is expressed not in big smiles, but in resourcefulness. Positive people look at a problem, accept it, and start looking for a solution.

7. Run With a Star Crowd

It's rare to find a star who regularly hangs out with non-stars. Typically, stars gather other stars around them, both at home and at work. If your so-called star is regularly hanging out with your toxic jerk, you should be suspicious. Part of the reason that stars are stars is that their "herd" is comprised of stars, too. We all become an average of the five people closest to us.

Excellence often comes in pockets. In grade school, the great athletes join the same herd, as do the great students, the great artists and actors, the great musicians, the great mechanics, and the great comics. Failure also comes in pockets. The terrible students, the partiers, the drug users, and the criminals hang out together, too. Things don't change much when we grow up.

As the Bible says, "As iron sharpens iron, so one person sharpens another" (Proverbs 27:17 NIV). Whether you're being sharpened or dulled all depends on what herd you choose to be part of.

8. Bloom Where They've Been Planted

A great way to identify a star is to look for a person who is blooming where he's been planted. If he's doing a great job where he is, and you would rehire him in a second if you had to do it all over again, you've got yourself a star.

That said, there are two types of stars: Some are great at their current job (they're blooming where they've been planted) and have the ability to move up in the organization and take on more. Others are great at what they do and should stay in their role permanently. They occupy what I call a "legacy" position.

Just because your star isn't promotable doesn't mean he can't claim star status. Those who are promotable show a desire for more, and clearly have the skill, leadership ability, and intelligence to get there. Both kinds are stars. The problem comes when people in legacy positions get promoted beyond their level of ability. In one stroke, you've lost a star and gained a non-star. This isn't a win.

I once had a meeting with a middle-aged man who was a gifted mechanic. He loved what he did, but felt that his career should have more forward momentum. With the help of his wife, he had drawn up a document detailing why he should be considered as a candidate to lead his large team of mechanics. His reasons were that he had been at the company for a long time, was the right age, and could fix every piece of equipment on the worksite.

After he made his case, I asked, "When you come home from work and you've had a great day, what were you doing that day?" He responded that his best days were when he was covered in grease, solving a complex mechanical problem that required a creative solution. So then I asked, "How about when you've had a draining day and gone home exhausted? What were you doing on *that* day?" He replied that draining days were the ones when he had to deal with customers or with interpersonal conflicts with other team members.

The job that he (or maybe his wife) thought he should have was one that incorporated all the elements that comprised a terrible day for him. Promoting him into a leadership position would clearly not have been a win—for him or for the company.

This person was in a great legacy role. He was brilliant at what he did. He was energized by his job, and he got better at it every day.

9. Track Record of Success

This is one of the surest signs of a star. When we're young, we bounce around and try a few things before we find our place in the world. That involves some bumps and scrapes, and sometimes means that we have gaps in our resume, or places that we tried that didn't work out. Student life, for instance, is transient, and student resumes may include multiple jobs.

Down times are golden opportunities for companies to rid themselves of non-stars. When sales are slow and someone has to go, the non-star goes first. For this reason, stars don't display a pattern of being laid off or "restructured," or of finding themselves in positions they have to leave because they couldn't find a way to overcome the obstacles in their way and make a success of things.

Though these things can happen to anyone—even stars—a resume dominated by these sorts of characteristics should be a red flag to you. More often, stars win everywhere they've been and are pulled from job to job without ever handing out a resume or seeking new work. When you're great, people all around you take note, and want to pull you out of your current job so that you can work for them.

10. Respected by Colleagues

Stars are transparent people who always show their true colors. They say what they believe to be true, and don't put on different masks depending on the situation they're in or the people they're with.

Whereas it's hard to fool your lateral colleagues, and virtually impossible to fool your direct reports, it's almost child's play to pull the wool over the eyes of the boss. This happens all the time; it's one of the great games that goes on in business. Everyone has something to gain (or lose) from the boss, so non-stars may engage in the dark arts of spin and flattery when the boss is around. Stars, however, avoid this type of deceit and, in doing so, earn the respect of their colleagues.

I was once a part of a good team that had a mis-hire forcibly injected into it by the boss, who met the man by chance on a plane. After only a few days, the mis-hire was both disliked and disrespected by his colleagues and subordinates, but because his core competence was spinning to and flattering the boss, he remained.

One day, out of the blue in a management meeting, to the amazement and disgust of his colleagues, the mis-hire publicly presented the boss with a trophy. It was 3 feet high and topped with a winged woman whose arms were held aloft in victory. On the base of the trophy was the boss's name emblazoned under the title "MVP." He then gave a speech about how great the boss was, elaborating on his real and imagined virtues for an extended time. The craziest thing about this bizarre situation was that the boss bought it, waxing eloquent about finding someone who finally understood the business! Only after the outcry from the rank and file became impossible to ignore was the flatterer finally dismissed.

People Action Steps

- Make a list of every key person on your team. Ask the four questions about each one, and answer them honestly.
- Make a commitment to yourself that you will be able to answer "yes" to each of the four questions within 18 months.

In Summary

You can discover whether or not you have stars on your team by asking four simple questions about each one:

1. If you could do it all over again, would you rehire her?
2. Does he take your stress away?
3. How would you feel if she quit?
4. What if everyone in the organization was just like him?

In addition, all stars have certain attitudes in common, regardless of their profession: maturity, passion, drive, integrity, reliability, and positivity. Stars also run with a star crowd, bloom where they've been planted, have a track record of success, and earn the respect of their colleagues.

Distill the Right Attitudes— and Make Them Stick

"A bunch of guys take off their ties and coats, go into a motel room for three days, and put a bunch of friggin' words on a piece of paper—and then go back to business as usual."

—John Rock, former maverick
manager at General Motors

Core people who have been around for a long time don't really need a list of rules to keep them on track. They already know what your company attitudes are; likely, they played a big part in creating your culture. You only need to formally define them when you start growing, because people who are new to the team have no idea what makes your company special. They need someone to tell them how "things are done around here."

These expectations of behavior go by all sorts of names, including core values, rules of engagement, house rules, shared values, company pillars, and more. Don't get hung up on the terminology. Focus on discovering the behaviors that make for successful hires in your company. We're going to use the term *right attitudes,* but please customize this to whatever works for you.

Think of your company's right attitudes as the circular ripples created when a rock is thrown into a still pond. The first few rings of ripples are very clear. The 10th ripple though, is faint. And the 20th, well, it can hardly be seen. That's why the new people need the attitudes to be spelled out: because they weren't around when the rock was first thrown and the initial ripples were made.

Having these attitudes formalized for everyone to see is important, because adherence to them is the biggest indicator of whether an employee will succeed or fail at your company. "Hey!" you cry. "That's totally subjective! It's not fair! It should just be about getting the work done, not about living by some subjective list of attitudes!"

If we were all robots, that would be a fair critique, and people would be judged only by completely objective criteria. But here in the human world, when an employee's attitude isn't right, that person doesn't work out. The absence of the right attitude isn't as subjective as you might think, either. Bad attitudes are quickly and easily sniffed out by you and everyone else on the team.

We've all observed this to be true from first-hand experience, but it's also borne out by hard data. Leadership IQ, a global leadership training and research company, studied 5,247 new hires made by hiring managers from 312 public, private, business, and healthcare organizations. Collectively these managers hired more than 20,000 employees during the study period. The study showed that 46 percent of new hires failed within 18 months; 89 percent of the time it was for attitudinal reasons and only 11 percent of the time for lack of skill.[1]

Why Defining Right Attitudes Is So Important to Your Company

Functioning in today's workplace is like white-water rafting, not sculling in a placid lake. Sculling is orderly. A perfectly unified team sits politely in their tiny craft, rowing in perfect synchronization. The coxswain sits at the back and shouts the orders. There's no talking back. Everyone listens and does precisely what they're told to do.

This is the perfect picture of what ideal work cultures of the past aspired to look like. Executives of the 1980s wept with joy reading about Japanese 20-year plans in which every possible permutation of the future was anticipated like a beautiful business ballet. Each member of the troupe did what he was told. Then the Japanese economy went into a 25-year tailspin, and the gurus began to think again.

White-water rafting is something quite different. Everyone is holding on for dear life as the zodiac careens madly, occasionally giving one person a blast of ice cold water in the face and bucking off that unlucky passenger in an unexpected lurch to starboard. There's no way to shout every order, and in any case, no one could hear them if you tried.

Our workplaces today are a bit like white-water rafting. Things are changing so quickly, and business is happening at such a break-neck pace that in today's white-water work environment, everyone needs to know the rules *before* getting in the boat so they'll know how to behave when the confusion hits. Here's a famous story from the past that illustrates this concept.

In 1805, the English fought the combined Spanish and French navies in what became famous as the Battle of Trafalgar. The English had fewer ships and poorer armaments; what proved to be Vice Admiral Horatio Nelson's winning strategy was his adoption of what was, at the time, a radically unorthodox culture. He built the original "Band of Brothers."

The Spanish and French built a culture of obedience. Ship captains were ordered to enter the battle and look to the all-knowing admiral's flagship for the signal flags that would tell them what to do in every circumstance. Nelson, on the other hand, built a culture of mutual respect and devotion. Although he had a carefully planned battle strategy, Nelson knew that everything would change once the enemy was engaged, so he remarked to his men, "No captain can do very wrong if he places his ship alongside that of the enemy," freeing his captains to use their own judgment once combat began.

The battle proved to be a deafening, smoke-filled scene of carnage and destruction. Trying to glimpse a far-away flag on the peak of a distant mast was impossible. The French and Spanish were confused, and the English capitalized on the chaos. The battle ended with every single Spanish and French ship burned, destroyed, or sunk, while the English didn't lose a single ship. Nelson secured the seas for the English for the next 100 years, and won his place in history at the top of Nelson's Column in Trafalgar Square in the heart of London, surrounded by four lions sculpted from the melted metal of his enemy's guns.

If your team is clear on what attitudes are expected from them, and all are rowing in the same direction, you will dominate any industry, anytime, anywhere.

How to Identify Your Right Attitudes

The first step is to define exactly which attitudes are important in your workplace. These will relate to what your company does. A company that offers grief counseling will obviously have right attitudes that are different from those chosen by a machine shop. An accounting office will be different again. Here are some simple suggestions for discovering them.

List the Traits of Your Best Employee

Think of a real-life employee. What is it about her that makes you and others love her performance? What are the qualities that make her so special? Is it her cleanliness or the way she treats her coworkers or the amount she's able to get done? Maybe it's the passion she brings to her work or her accuracy and thoroughness. Write a list of these qualities, and be as specific as possible in your description.

Now ask yourself if the things you love about this person have wider application to your work force. Are these the attitudes that many or perhaps all of your most successful employees share? If so, you have found one of your company's right attitudes.

The fact that you love the behavior of these stars suggests that they're living out something that's important to you on a deeper level. When you examine what they're doing right, you'll find valuable clues to outline your company's important right attitudes.

Reflect on What Makes You Angry

You'll know you've hit on a right attitude when the thought of someone violating it makes you angry. Think back to the times that you've felt angry at work over the last six months. Was your anger sparked because a right attitude was being violated? If so, your anger can be a major clue to finding what your right attitudes are.

I learned this principle one hot summer afternoon from the management team of a very successful company as we tried to puzzle out the company's right attitudes. We'd agreed on two, but still, something was missing, although we couldn't put our finger on just what it was. As the afternoon wore on, the group was slowly going numb, so in desperation, I turned to one of the owners, and asked her, "When was the last time you got *really mad* at someone?"

Without hesitation, she described how she went on a tear with a leader over his treatment of one of his reports. "He had no respect, and I *will not* stand for that in this company," she emphatically declared. Her passion around this issue was real and raw, and caused light bulbs to turn on all over the room. "Respect for all" became their final right attitude.

Some clients are furious when they hear a customer has been treated with indifference, see a poor-quality product being sent out, or observe an employee who shows no passion for the job. Look to your anger for clues about what your right attitudes are.

Identify the Attitudes That Are Currently Being Lived Out

You don't make up right attitudes out of thin air. They are behaviors that are already being lived out every day in your company. Your right attitudes define what makes your culture special and unique. They aren't aspirational; they're living and real. You shouldn't have to search far to find them because employees should be displaying them on a regular basis.

Typically, though, that's not how this exercise is approached. Usually official statements are put together by a committee because someone at the top fell for the latest management fad. Usually they're wordy and lofty—and meaningless.

Here's how official statements often function in real companies: A few years ago, I was a groomsman at a friend's wedding. As a thank you, he gave me a watch that was privately labeled with the name of a popular retailer. It stopped working within the month. When I brought it to the store, the salesperson glanced at it indifferently and said in his most off-putting manner, "Yeah, lots of those have broken, but we don't take them back, if that's what you're thinking."

We debated the merits of this line of thinking for a couple of fruitless minutes, until a corporate plaque above his head caught my eye. It read: *"Our Creed: To give you such outstanding quality, value, service, and guarantee that we may be worthy of your high esteem."*

Wow. How noble. I almost teared up. I drew my new friend's attention to his company's creed, and remarked, "I've got to tell you, the quality, value, service, and guarantee that I'm experiencing right now is not evoking my highest esteem."

Without blinking, he gave me a customers-are-so-dim look, shook his head, and shot back, "That's just a sign!"

You've seen official statements like these hanging on the wall. They're meant to be inoffensive and make everyone happy, and, as a result, they have no teeth. It's not that any of the values proclaimed on them are wrong. They're all good things. They're just *irrelevant*. These statements could be hung in the boardrooms of any competitor, and no one would blink an eye. They would be just as vanilla, unnoticed, and meaningless there.

Everyone knows these framed statements have nothing to do with their actual lives. People don't care about what's written on the walls, but about what happens in the halls.

Your right attitude statements, however, are going to be different, because they're going to be specific, short, and memorable, and have real teeth. They're going to be one of the main HR tools for your whole company. You will hire, onboard, evaluate, praise, and discipline based in large part on your right attitudes.

These attitudes will make your stars happy because good behaviour will be enforced and rewarded, and help your non-stars get better because bad behavior will be called out, too. In short, they will become the measuring stick that everyone will live by, and be evaluated by, whether it's the CEO or the newest entry-level hire.

If you were to interview your best people about what they value in the company, they would likely touch on some of the attitudes that already exist that make your company special. Your company's right attitudes are being lived out every day. It's your job to identify them. Ask yourself, "What has made us win up to now?"

Analyze the Attitudes That Have Been Violated

A good employment fit can be thought of as the three legs of a stool, represented by competence, character, and chemistry. All three components are important, but the main reason—by a country mile—that people don't work out is chemistry, which is another way of saying right attitudes.

Think of someone that you let go in the past year or two. What offense did he commit that led to his termination? Was it a question of competence or character? Or was it something else?

If you have chemistry with someone, he "gets it." He already shares your way of thinking, and he values what you and your team value. He just *feels* like a fit.

Skills can be taught for the most part, but it's very difficult to teach attitudes to people, because attitudes represent what they really believe. The challenge is to find people who *already* share your attitudes—not find people and then try to teach them to believe what you believe. Attitudes can be shaped in young people to some degree, but if a person's been on the planet for a while, their attitudes are usually set.

Thinking about people that you've let go in the past year or two will help you discover what your company's right attitudes really are. If you've let someone go because he wasn't a good fit, but you can't point to the attitude from your current list that he violated, you may need to go back to the drawing board to find out which right attitude has not been discovered.

You can approach this dynamic from another direction. Ask yourself, "If a person was to repeatedly violate one of our right attitudes, would I eventually fire him over it?" This is a pivotal question, because it forces you to ask what attitudes are *really* important to you, which parts of your company culture you're willing to defend and which parts don't matter as much to you. You know you're serious if you're willing to fire over it. If not, it's probably not an attitude that's critical to success for you.

Your commitment to firing over repeated "soft skill" violations transforms your right attitudes from meaningless words into ideas that people believe in, commit to, and strive to live up to.

What Right Attitudes Do You Want Your Company to Retain a Century From Now?

Attitudes that are important to you don't change over time. Your strategy will evolve, as will your products, services, and customer base, but those attitudes should be the same forever. For that reason, give yourself some time to discover them.

When you choose your right attitudes and put them to paper, write them in pencil. Once you've lived with them for six months to a year, you'll have a good idea if they're really core to your business. There's a good chance that some will feel like duplicates, or upon reflection, some won't feel as core to you as they did when you wrote them down. It takes time to sort out right attitudes. Once you've tried them out for a few months and everyone agrees that they are the right ones, carve them in stone and strive to embody them. Nothing is more important to your culture than leaders who "walk the talk" all the time.

How to Make Your Right Attitudes "Sticky"

When I brought up the idea of developing right attitudes with one client company, the leadership team objected on the grounds that they had already completed a values-discovery exercise; in fact, they had identified 10 core values, and had them beautifully written (in calligraphy), framed, and hung on the wall of the very boardroom in which we were having our discussion. I calmly walked to the framed statement, removed it from the fastener that held it in place, and set it down, facing the wall. Then I turned to the team and asked them to recite the values.

Crickets.

The silence hung heavy in the air until one person remembered something about being stewards of the environment. After another pregnant pause, someone else remembered "giving back to the community." There was another lengthy silence as the top leaders of the company exchanged glances, straining to remember just one of the 10 things that they all had agreed were the most important values to the business.

I'm sure they were deeply committed to the values, they just couldn't remember what any of them were! After sharing a good laugh, we proceeded to re-shape their values statement to a format that was a bit more real—and a lot more memorable.

You may absolutely nail the right attitudes that are alive in your organization, and still find that people struggle to remember what they are. If they aren't memorable, they aren't going to be of much use to anyone.

The acid test for memorable or "sticky" right attitudes is this: will your newest, youngest employee remember them after hearing them only once?

Don't be worried about wordsmithing these statements until they're grammatically perfect. You aren't trying to get a checkmark from an imaginary business professor, and grammatical perfection isn't the goal; it might even hamper the stickiness of your values. Instead, worry about how to make the attitudes simple so that everyone can easily remember them. Following are five useful tricks.

Remember the "Rule of Three"

The human brain has an ability to hold three things in focus at one time. When there are four or five or 12 things to focus on, clarity melts into confusion. If your company attitudes are going to be used in daily life, they need to be sticky, so focus on discovering no more than three right attitudes. Usually these involve something about work ethic, something about interacting with the team, and something about the frame of mind they show up with each day.

Thomas Jefferson used the Rule of Three in writing the Declaration of Independence: "Life, liberty, and the pursuit of happiness" are among the most important words in all of American, perhaps human, history. The U.S. Air Force has three laws for surviving captivity: fellowship with other prisoners, survive, and return with honor. Steve Jobs used the Rule of Three in almost every public presentation he made at Apple. For instance, he proclaimed that the iPad 2 would be "thinner, lighter, and faster" than the original. Movie theaters and restaurants have built businesses based on food choices of "small, medium, and large." The Rule of Three is all around us.

Consider an Acronym

Acronyms can help make your right attitudes sticky. Maybe the name of your company can be used to build the acronym. Once you have chosen your values, you may be able to find a way for them to spell a word that's easy to remember. CREW Marketing Partners did this in reverse and used their core values (character, relationships, execution, wow) to name the company.

Resist the temptation to shape your right attitudes around a cool word that seems like the perfect fit. The attitudes are more important than how they are presented.

Attempt Alliteration

Starting all of your attitudes with the same letter isn't a guaranteed recipe for stickiness, but it doesn't hurt.

A client who runs a chain of restaurants worked hard to make his right attitudes memorable, or "sticky." Finally, he chose three words: win, wash, and wow.

Win referred to winning together. If something worked for a franchisee but not the home office, it wouldn't pass the right attitudes test. If management was happy and employees weren't, things had to be re-examined.

Wash was a short way to remember the axiom "No one is too good to wash toilets." That meant that when the restaurant closed for the day, every person helped clean until the job was done, regardless of rank. Managers might wash dishes or scrub toilets, or servers might clean greasy stovetops. This contributed to an egalitarian, team-based culture.

Wow referred to the goal of having every customer say "Wow!" about all aspects of their experience in the restaurant. That included the cleanliness of the premises, the friendliness of the staff, and the presentation and taste of the food.

Best of all, a new employee could remember "win, wash, wow" after hearing it the first time. It was really sticky.

Adopt Common Sayings

Adopting phrases that are already in common use in the business is a really great way to communicate shared values. The fact that they're already well known is an indicator that they may express something that's really important. Phrases like *get 'er done, watch the pennies,* and *don't let the rules make you stupid* convey meaning that everyone already gets. If a saying is already in use and it reflects something that's core, by all means use it.

At the end of this chapter I've included some real-life examples of right attitudes used by real companies, many of which are sayings that were already alive in their businesses. Look at these to spark your thinking.

Tell Company Legends

Stories are the best way to make right attitudes sticky. Rather than just telling employees to "keep your promises," share a story about the lengths a real person has gone to in order to keep a promise. A story is memorable, conveys emotion, and illustrates how you want your employees to act. Reason (the words you hang on the wall) persuades, but emotion (the attitude stories you tell) motivates. A powerful story teaches your right attitudes better than any other method you can use.

Imagine a Nordstrom employee hearing the following story (which I heard from a participant in a business class I was teaching):

I once drove from Vancouver to Seattle to buy a suit from Nordstrom for my daughter's wedding. Nordstrom is known for having amazing customer service. When I got the suit home, I found—to my shock—that they had given me the wrong pair of pants. They were the wrong colour, and they didn't fit. I immediately phoned the store, and they said, "No problem, we'll have someone drive those pants up to Vancouver for you right away." A few hours later, I shared a glass of lemonade with a Nordstrom employee on my back deck.

Telling this story to a new employee would teach her everything she would need to know about Nordstrom's above-and-beyond customer service. Plus, this story has a built-in bonus, as explained by my class participant when he concluded the story: "The great thing for Nordstrom is that I've told that story over and over and over again. They really got their money's worth in advertising!"

Time to Brainstorm

Attitudes are different for every business. Here's a list of some real-life right attitudes used by real clients. Pick the three that resonate with you, and then customize them, or invent your own:

- Get 'er done.
- Work passionately.
- Respect others.
- Continuous improvement.
- Professionalism.
- Do more with less.
- Win together, not alone.
- Tidy and clean.
- Open and transparent.
- No surprises.
- Own it!
- Raise the bar.
- Always positive.
- Trustworthy—do the right thing and do things right.
- Obey the golden rule.
- Think win-win.
- Fanatical customer service.
- Invest wisely.
- Focus on results.
- No one's too good to wash toilets.
- Keep our promises.
- Be a lifter, not a leaner.

- Relationships first.
- Your attitude determines your altitude.
- House of "Yes" (as long as it's not immoral or illegal, make the customer happy).
- Watch the pennies.
- Make everything a "WOW."
- Always do the right thing.
- Accountable for our successes and setbacks.
- Do it now!
- G-rated culture.
- Make a customer's day.
- Always be busy.
- Think it through.
- Customer relationships first.
- Find a better way.
- Superb quality work.
- Salary maker, not salary taker.
- High performance.
- Trusting relationships.

A retail store is likely going to have different right attitudes from a professional services firm or a quick-serve restaurant, but defining them helps each employee know what behaviors are expected of them and which ones will get them in trouble.

People Action Steps

- Assemble your leadership team and work through the previous list of attitudes.
- Choose and/or customize three of them that describe your company's right attitudes.
- Test them out for six months by telling stories that illustrate them, using them in hiring interviews, and referring to them when giving praise or correction.
- Once you and your team are sure they're on point, put the right attitudes on the wall and "walk the talk."

In Summary

When your company is growing, you need to discover and define your three right attitudes. They are the behaviors that employees live out that make your company special and different from your competitors; they define which behaviors are and are not acceptable at your company.

You discover them by:

- Making a list of the behaviors that typify your very best employees.
- Reflecting on what makes you angry. Your temper is ignited when right attitudes are violated.
- Looking for those right attitudes that are lived out in your company every day. Values are discovered, not invented.

- Reflecting on those people who haven't worked out. What attitudes did they violate that ended in their termination?
- Anticipating what attitudes your company will retain in a century.

Here's how to make the attitudes sticky:

- Obey the Rule of Three. People can't hold more than three things in focus, so limit the number of attitudes you choose.
- Consider an acronym. Spell out a word using the first letters of your right attitudes.
- Attempt alliteration. Have all of your attitudes begin with the same letter.
- Adopt common sayings. Use sayings that are already in common use that everyone already understands.
- Tell company legends. Think of stories that illustrate your attitudes better than any words ever could. Tell the stories over and over again.
- Choose and/or customize your company attitudes from the list provided in the chapter.

4

Take Action With Your Underperformers

"The toughest decisions in organizations are people decisions—hiring, firing, promotion, etc. These are the decisions that receive the least attention and are the hardest to 'unmake.'"

—Peter Drucker, management
consultant, educator, and author

Getting the right people in the key seats is your most important job as leader. It's so important that you must summon the discipline to resist making quick hires in these roles, because mistakes at this level are costly. You need the *right* people, not just *good* people. If you're not sure that a person is right, you need to pass.

It's easy to see the sense in showing more discipline when you hire, but what about the people who already work for you? The truth is, most leaders resist doing an honest review of their teams. It's a tough assignment because it's very subjective and often involves factors unrelated to their actual work.

In *Good to Great*, the landmark study of companies that beat the general market (and their closest competitors) by a cumulative total stock return of at least three times for 15 consecutive years, Jim Collins found that every company that went from good performance to great performance took the same six steps on their path to greatness.

In every case, the first two steps on the journey were about getting a critical mass of right people in the company. That meant first, finding "level five" key leaders (those possessing a combination of humility and drive) and second, getting "the right people on the bus and the wrong people off the bus."[1]

It's pretty obvious that it is really important to attract and retain stars, though it's often forgotten that it's just as important to identify underperformers and hold them accountable to getting the results they need to achieve—and to take action with them if they can't or won't do so. That said, actually holding people accountable is like drinking poison for many people leaders. Why is it so difficult, and what we can do about it?

Common Excuses for Giving Underperformers a Pass

In most companies, there's an assumption that underperformers, particularly ones who have been with the company for a long time, are safe—even untouchable. There are also huge emotional barriers to acting on non-stars.

Here are some of the most common rationales that I hear from clients:

- "She's been here for 20 years, and while she underperforms, we've become friends and shared so much of our lives together, that I couldn't possibly hold her accountable now."
- "He's a struggler and always will be, but at least he can be counted on to show up in the morning. He's better than having no one at all."
- "We could never afford the cost of litigation and severance if we let her go."
- "We could never find the time to replace him when we're this busy."
- "She's been here so long that, while she underperforms, she serves the valuable role of 'historian' and 'keeper of the values.'"
- "Sure, he's weak at his job, but our kids play soccer together and we're neighbors."
- "I'm sorry but I can't have a tough talk with a single mom who has three kids to support."
- "If I were to fire him, I think he might commit suicide because he could never find another job."
- "Our culture is different than the ones in the books. Acting on underperformers would destroy the family feel of our company."

These are all real reasons that I've heard from leaders about why they don't take action. Though firing may not be the answer, something needs to be done to challenge, reposition, or replace non-stars. These situations are causing you and your teammates real problems and need to be dealt with so that everyone can move forward.

False Assumptions Prop Up Excuses

Let's look at three common assumptions that underlie most of our reasons for inaction.

It Isn't "Nice" to Confront People About Their Performance

Most people don't take action on non-stars because they really believe that it isn't a nice thing to do. But is it *really* nice to ignore poor performance?

First, consider the people who have to work with and for these people. They are the ones who have to put up with their difficult behavior, do extra work to cover for them, and live in a business that offers them less opportunity than it should. These are the people who choose to work elsewhere because they have to endure the non-star every day. Are you being nice to *them* by ignoring subpar performance from your non-stars? Sometimes, non-stars can make everyone else's life harder because they don't pull their weight and force others to do it for them. They can make the lives of those around them downright miserable, and when they're finally dealt with, people all around them cheer.

Second, consider the company. Non-stars make poor mentors because they teach bad habits to their protégés. If they have influence over hiring decisions, they always choose to hire people who are weaker than they are; they find stars too eager by far. They attract lower-quality customers and turn off great ones. They make your company less competitive and therefore less safe for all those who depend on the business to feed their families. That's not nice!

Ignoring a Performance Deficit Is Nicer Than the Alternative

Now let's think about the underperformer. Is it nice to them to ignore their performance deficit? On the contrary—ignoring underperformance is one of the cruelest things you can do to a subordinate. The cruelty is unintentional, but I've seen the following scenario played out again and again.

Times are good, and while the underperformer doesn't bring a lot of value to the company, she's nice enough, and so you ignore her results and bury the issues. When things get tough, though, it's a different story, and it may become financially impossible to continue to hang on to this person.

When you're deciding who to lay off, it's always going to be the underperformer first. When she hears the news, she feels angry, bitter, and betrayed, because her reviews were always satisfactory, and now she is being let go while others, maybe people junior to her, are being retained. Worst of all, this may happen when she is in her 40s or 50s, a difficult time for her to make a change. That's not being nice.

The Underperformer Has Limited Alternatives

We sometimes assume that a non-star won't have any other option if we let him go. But this might short-change your underperformer. Have you considered the possibility that your non-star might be a star somewhere else and that a push to make a change is exactly what he needs? Here's a list of some now-famous people who were fired at least once in their careers, and the reasons they were let go:

Employee	Reason for Dismissal
Steve Jobs (Apple co-founder)	Being difficult
Bill Watterson (*Calvin and Hobbes* creator)	(as a political cartoonist) Not good enough
Walt Disney (animation, theme park mogul)	Lacked imagination; no good ideas
Bill Belichick (NFL coach)	(from the Cleveland Browns) Owner wasn't happy with him
Michael Bloomberg (former mayor of NYC)	Downsized when his company was sold
Bernie Marcus (founder of Home Depot)	Laid off after the company he worked for was sold
J.K. Rowling (author of the *Harry Potter* series)	Not doing her secretarial work; working on stories instead
Michael Jordan (NBA player)	Not good enough for the Washington Wizards

Robert Redford (actor)	(from Standard Oil) Lazy and sloppy
Anna Wintour (editor of *Vogue*)	Too edgy to be a junior fashion editor
Lee Iacocca (chairman of Chrysler)	Personality clash with the owner
Jerry Seinfeld (comedian)	(from the sitcom *Benson*) No reason given; when he showed up for work, his part was missing from the script (and he got the message)
Oprah Winfrey (TV personality)	Too emotionally involved to be a TV news reporter
Elvis (singer)	Told by the manager of the Grand Ole Opry that he should return to truck driving
Truman Capote (author)	(as a copyboy for the *New Yorker*) For offending poet Robert Frost
Mark Cuban (billionaire)	Failing to do the morning opening in the store he worked at
Madonna (singer)	Squirting donut jelly on a customer at Dunkin' Donuts
Thomas Edison (inventor)	Spilling acid on the floor while experimenting with an invention that had nothing to do with his work

Some of these seem crazy (Walt Disney not creative enough—seriously?), but most were crucial moments of redirection for young people who needed to rethink their areas of strength and weakness, and ask themselves if they were in the right job; in short, these hard times were blessings in disguise.

Imagine if Madonna had gone on to be regional *manager* at Dunkin' Donuts? Where would she be today? What if Standard Oil had put up with Robert Redford's sloppy work as a manual laborer? Where would he be today? Or if J.K. Rowling's poor performance as a secretary had been tolerated by her superiors? Harry Potter might be just another failed magician.

You may be thinking, "Believe me, my non-star isn't going to win an Academy Award anytime soon!" That may be so, but it's quite possible—even likely—that she will go on to find a place that fits her values or ignites her passions in a way that you and your company don't. Who knows? Maybe you'll work for her one day in a company she'll go on to found.

Facing Up to Non-Stars: A True Case Study

Early in my coaching career, I met a young man named Dan. He was working in sales in a family business founded and operated by his father, and he was being groomed for leadership. He hoped to one day run the business. Dan was (and is) focused, determined, and a ton of fun.

When he finally took the business over and sat in the "big chair," his dad gave him (and me) some advice. It sounded something like this: "Dan, I've had 35 years to build my team, and now it's your turn. Your biggest job will be building a team of your own that can take the business to the new levels that you want to reach. You have my support in doing whatever you feel you need to do."

So, we began what proved to be a long journey by looking at each person in every key role and asking the first essential question detailed in Chapter 2: If we could do it all over again, would we hire this person? As we went through the list, it got depressing, because again and again the answer was no.

These mental exercises are fine in theory, or in a classroom, but you can't just re-adjust, repurpose, and, as a last resort, swap out each key seat until you have a star in every role, can you? It's just not done. You can't rock the boat like that. Or can you?

After much deliberation, that's exactly what Dan decided to do. He sat with every key person and respectfully outlined his expectations. He held accountability meetings, making everyone's responsibilities clear to the entire group and assuming they would be completed. If leaders showed a pattern of not getting core tasks done, it became obvious to the rest of the team, and Dan quietly, firmly, and kindly held each one to account.

Some employees hated this new level of expectation and transparency, and found other jobs. Others (his best people) loved it because it meant that things were getting done and the company was moving ahead to a bright new future.

It was a long road, but Dan's determination paid off. Today, he oversees a culture that is unprecedented in its openness and productivity. He has many new star players. He's also retained some long-termers who wanted to perform at a high level. Some of them adjusted or changed roles, and some stepped up their game to a new level.

When I look at the top 20 or so key seats in that business now, all of them are filled with star players. Once Dan completed those staff changes, the business started to grow—fast.

Today Dan's company is about five times the size it was when he took over. However, the business began to dramatically change with the addition of only three key team members. These stars brought with them new attitudes and ideas, and set a new bar for performance in every respect.

How about your business? Are you treading water, content with the unhappy status quo? Are your key leaders setting the pace? If you could hire each one all over again, would you? The most important key to human motivation is pretty simple: People follow the example of their leaders.

People Action Steps

- Rate your current team from best to worst, as if you were the coach of a hockey team.
- Be clear on who your lowest and highest performers are.
- If you think it's not nice to avoid underperformance, change your thinking on this matter.

In Summary

The first steps in your transition from a good company to a great one are getting the right people and putting them in the right roles. Although we understand that we need to be careful when making hires, dealing with our current team is another matter. Most leaders resist rating their team honestly and acting on underperformers. The reason leaders resist is mostly because they want to be nice. Allowing underperformance, though, isn't being nice to anybody, including:

- Those who have to work with the underperformer. Someone has to pull the extra weight, and it's not fun for colleagues who have to do the extra work. In addition, underperformers make poor mentors, and turn off your best customers and staff.
- The company. Underperformers make the company less competitive, less profitable, and therefore less secure (because it is forced to offer less opportunity to all of the great people).
- The underperformer himself. He may be an underperformer at your company, but release may provide an opportunity where he does fit and can fully engage. Often underperformers are retained until circumstances force a change when they're least equipped to go through it— in their 40s and 50s.

5

Use the Star Chart to Rate Your Current Team

"There are three types of baseball players. Those that make it happen, those that watch it happen, and those that wonder what's happening."

—Tommy Lasorda, former MLB player and manager of the Los Angeles Dodgers

I've said something like this to many leaders: "One hour from now, we're all going to be crystal clear about what you need to do in order to solve 90 percent of your people problems—permanently. We're also going to have a clear, actionable development plan for every member of your team. You are now starting your journey toward having virtually no HR problems. We'll get this done *in one hour.*"

Inevitably reactions vary. Some are doubtful; some are hopeful; some are highly skeptical, thinking about how adept their worst performers are at evading the accountability noose so that once this "program" has run its course, they can settle back into their lives as gentlemen-of-leisure or playground bully or even toxic jerk.

But I can assure you that my opening remarks are no exaggeration. This is the beginning of your journey toward eliminating 90 percent of your people problems. I know this because I've watched it work in many organizations, both profit and non-profit.

What the Star Chart Does (and Doesn't) Measure

The Star Chart is a tool that brings objectivity and clarity to the people issues that currently feel subjective and cloudy. Evaluating people's performance by quadrant is not a new idea, and certainly not one that I invented. In fact, variations on this theme have been around for years—largely because it works!

The Star Chart is an incredible tool that will change how you think about leading and developing your team.

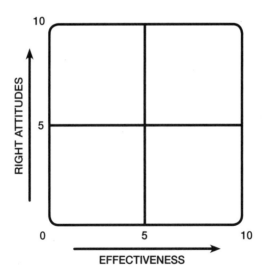

It's important to keep in mind that the Star Chart doesn't attempt to help you place a value on *people*. The Star Chart only measures a person's *effectiveness in her current role*. It does not measure whether she is a good or bad human being. She may be a great family member, nice person, good parent, involved softball coach, caring friend, and so on. You're not judging her as a person; you just want to assess how well she fits into your company and how effective she is at her job.

How the Star Chart Works

You'll plot each of your key employees, one at a time, on the same Star Chart. You may have 50 people to plot. Use different colors, initials, and a large sheet of paper. Write small! Each time, think about a person's performance in his current role.

The vertical (right attitudes) axis covers all of the "soft," more subjective aspects of your employee's contribution at work—what he's like to live alongside and how he does (or doesn't) embody the company's right attitudes. The horizontal (effectiveness) axis assesses the more objective question of how much actual work he gets done.

Plotting the Vertical Axis: Right Attitudes

We're now going to put the right attitudes we discovered in Chapter 3 to practical use, as a measuring stick for each employee's behavior. You will estimate how much of the time he spends living out those attitudes that are core to your company's culture.

Begin by estimating how much of his workday or week he spends living out the right attitudes, on a scale of one to 10. A person who scores a one on the vertical axis (and therefore is positioned on the bottom) would display the worst attitudes possible on the scale. A person who scores a 10 (and therefore is positioned on the top) would consistently display the best possible attitudes, with few or no slip-ups. A person who scores a five would be in the middle: half of the time living out those attitudes, or only living out some of them, and half of the time not.

What about employees who sometimes have wonderful attitudes but sometimes don't? Maybe the person you're grading typically has an exemplary outlook (embracing the right attitudes 90 to 95 percent of the time) from Monday afternoon to Wednesday, exhibits a moderately acceptable outlook (embracing right attitudes, say, 75 percent of the time) on Thursday, and is often a nightmare (embracing right attitudes in the 30- to 45-percent range) from Friday to Monday noon. But Tuesday and Wednesday, wow, he is great!

To put it in a different context, how would you feel if that person was your goalie: on fire every two games, okay for the next two, and a sieve for the last one? Would this track record make him a star? Probably not. Consistency matters. Consider *overall* behavior when you're doing your Star Chart plotting.

Once you've estimated the right attitudes score, plot it on the vertical axis.

Plotting the Horizontal Axis: Effectiveness

The horizontal axis measures a person's effectiveness in her current role. Estimate how much of her time in a given day or week is spent being productive in the role that she is currently being asked to fill.

Again, estimate a number from one to 10, and choose where she fits on the horizontal "effectiveness" axis. Remember: you're not measuring her value as a person, you're only measuring her effectiveness in the job she's doing right now. You are focusing on job performance only.

• • •

Now that you've thought through your scores, bring the results from the vertical axis and horizontal axis together, and see which box your employee is currently living in.

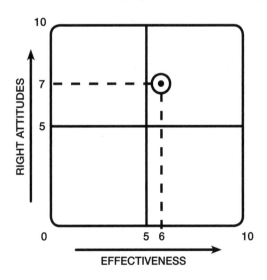

Explaining the Boxes

Finally, label the quadrants. Starting from the upper right and moving counter-clockwise: Box A contains your stars; Box B, your potential stars; Box C, your wrong fits; and Box D, your productive-but-difficult staff members. Chapters 8 to 11 provide detailed strategies for how to build an HR plan for each of these four groups of people. For now, your goal should simply be classification.

At times, you may be tempted to score a person at a five (or precisely on the line dividing one box from its neighbor). If you do so, follow the rule that says that anyone who scores exactly five automatically gets bumped down to a four (and therefore goes into the "lower" box or lesser category). In other words, someone on the horizontal axis between a star and potential star becomes the latter if they score a five. The idea here is to have clarity, and choosing five is usually a way of copping out so that no one needs to take any action.

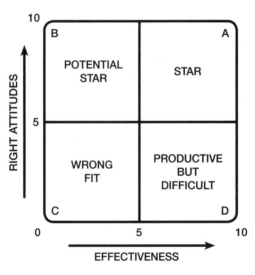

Repeat this process for each one of your team members until you have them all clearly plotted on the Star Chart.

Does the Star Chart Measure Promotability?

Let's be clear on another point. The Star Chart measures a person's effectiveness in his current role; it does *not* measure his promotability.

Say you own a retail store, and you need a greeter to hand out shopping carts and to smile and acknowledge every customer. Provided that your new hire has the right attitude and is handy with a drying towel when it rains, you have a star on your hands! Someday, he might go on to bigger things, but for now, he's doing what you need done and he's doing it well.

Let's move ahead a few months, and now your new employee has won everyone's heart. He's always cheerful and has a kind word for everybody. He's an inspiration. So when there's an opening to run a register, he's the obvious choice. Everyone loves him.

Soon it becomes apparent that he has no ability to deal with numbers. His register never balances and he's floundering. Even though he's got a great attitude, in this new role he moves back into the potential star box. And maybe because he knows he's doing a bad job, his attitude sags as well, and he sinks lower into the wrong fit box. He was a star as a greeter, but is not promotable to a cashier position.

How Are People Likely to Respond to the Star Chart?

Who loves report cards in high school? That's easy. The ones who think they're going to get good marks. And who hates them? The ones who think they're going to get bad marks.

Who loves tryouts for sports teams? The ones who've worked the hardest and know they're going to be among the best. Who hates them? The ones who think they might be cut.

This isn't a new or shocking idea. We live with performance expectations all our lives, and then abandon them when we enter our careers, just when the contributions we make matter most.

Your stars will love this process. Finally they'll be recognized for their superior contribution and will begin to see their workplace become happy and productive.

Your potential stars may be intimidated at first, but because their hearts are in the right place, they really do want the company and themselves to get better. Soon they'll be on board, getting coaching and training, or seeing their role adjusted so they can live in the star box, too.

Soon, the idea that everyone in the company is expected to live in the star box is just a fact of life. It's not debated or hated. It's obvious to everyone. If you work in any company, you have to try your best and have a good attitude, don't you? Obviously! Isn't this the assumption of every good person before they get into the workforce?

The people living in the bottom half of the Star Chart probably won't love this process, because it's going to challenge them to make some choices about how they want to approach their work. In fact, they'll likely fight the process, disparage it to their coworkers, or even refuse to take part in it at first.

While implementing the Star Chart, take heart. German philosopher Arthur Schopenhauer pioneered the idea of the Three Stages of Truth in the 19th century. He maintained that all truth passes through three stages. First, it is ridiculed. Second, it is violently opposed. Third, it is accepted as being self-evident. You'll find this to be true, too, as you begin using the Star Chart.

When you are implementing this or any new initiative in your business, ask yourself who will resist it or complain about it. Will it be the stars? If so, maybe you shouldn't be doing it. They're the people who care most and understand the business best. It's pretty important that they support your new, significant ideas.

If it's your non-stars (in other words, the ones who score low on the right attitudes axis and therefore live in the bottom half of the Star Chart) that hate the initiative, I wouldn't worry too much about it. Your goal is to make your workplace comfortable for the people who care the most and uncomfortable for those who care least.

The Star Chart in Practice

I once worked with a large firm whose leaders wanted to improve company morale and performance. We began by plotting every person in the company on a Star Chart. When this was done, we were concerned to see that at least one quarter of the company was classified as non-stars. The top half of the chart was pretty evenly distributed with names. After a lot of discussion about what was causing their morale and productivity problems, we made a commitment to have everyone in the star box within two years.

Management began by doing reviews with every person in the business, being respectful, kind, and clear about which box each person currently occupied. They encouraged their stars, and drew up plans with everyone else detailing how they could move into the star box.

The people who landed on the top half of the Star Chart were easy to deal with. Some of them just needed coaching or training, some needed a tweak to their job description so that they could focus more on their areas of strength, and some needed a long overdue heart-to-heart talk about their place on the Star Chart so that their legitimate concerns could be addressed.

For those on the bottom half of the Star Chart, their problems were deeper and not so easy to address. There was a great deal of pushback from this group. They took every opportunity to undermine the process. They talked quietly among themselves in lunchrooms and laughed with coworkers about the new management fad that, like the flu, would soon pass. When it didn't stop, they got more vocal, expressing their displeasure openly, even during interviews with management.

Despite this, leadership persisted and the process soon began yielding results. Longstanding issues came to the surface. Some people's roles were repositioned to take better advantage of their areas of strength, and some found different jobs and others were asked to leave. Everyone hired from that point on was vetted using a rigorous process to determine both attitudes and competence.

As they stuck to the process, positivity gained momentum. Finally, little more than two years after the initiative began, every single person in the business was plotted as a star. Coinciding with this milestone, the business hit unprecedented highs in profit and morale.

Once we had a culture of star players, I met with each employee team, explaining the Star Chart and our philosophy of building a great culture (a great culture is filled with stars; a terrible culture tolerates non-stars). The interesting thing was that team after team was positively enthusiastic about the company's commitment to ensuring that each person lived in that star box. Lots of stories were shared during these sessions about the misery of being forced to work with non-stars.

Good people want to work with other good people.

The Supreme Importance of Having Stars in Your Key Seats

In a survey published by *Harvard Business Review*, 13,000 senior managers and 112 companies were studied during a period of five years on the topic of building great managerial talent. The companies that performed best were those that took deliberate action to ensure that top-tier talent occupied the key seats in the business, and that underperformance triggered consequences. In two companies studied, star managers grew profits on average 105 percent, while non-star managers achieved no profit growth at all. The study points to something that all leaders know without having to read books or articles: Poor performers achieve poor results.

To me, the most illuminating finding of the study was that "only 16 percent of managers strongly agreed that their companies knew who the high and low performers were in the senior ranks."[1]

Though the respondents may have believed this to be the case, I don't buy it. *All* leaders know who their weakest and strongest players are. They just choose to not *act* on that knowledge, so it looks to their subordinates as if they're completely out of touch with reality and unaware of the most basic of team fundamentals: who is strong and who is weak.

If you were a hockey coach, the caliber of your players would not be a mystery, let alone to the average fan. You would have a list of your players based on performance, from best to worst. Each player would also know where he stood, based on his income, the ice time he received, and the points he put on the board. There are no secrets in that environment. Those who are most serious about winning are also the most serious about developing and deploying talent effectively.

People Action Steps

- Create a Star Chart, and plot all of your employees on the same Star Chart.
- Interview each employee, and tell them where they fit on the Star Chart.
- Don't be deterred by opposition from non-stars. Stick with the process.

In Summary

The Star Chart is a simple way to turn something that seems very subjective (grading your team) into something that is much more objective.

- Grade each employee according to how much she lives out your company's right attitudes in a typical week or month, on a scale from one to 10. Plot that number on the vertical axis.
- Assess each employee according to how productive each person is over the same time period, again on a scale from one to 10. Plot that number on the horizontal axis.
- Finally, plot the employee on the Star Chart, joining the two lines together. This will show you which box the employee fits in: star, potential star, wrong fit, or productive-but-difficult.

Your highest performers will love going through the process because their performance will finally be formally recognized. Your lowest performers may dislike the process and try to sabotage it, for similar reasons.

6

Dispel the People Myths That Most Affect Your Company

"If you think a weakness can be turned into a strength, I hate to tell you this, but that's another weakness."

—Jack Handy, author of
Deep Thoughts by Jack Handy

"The School for Animals" is a fable written by George Reavis in the 1940s and that has been retold in various forms many times since. It's a fun story illustrating some basic truths about assessing strengths and weaknesses. It goes like this.

Once upon a time, some animals decided to start a school. The teachers met and agreed to provide a standardized curriculum, consisting of swimming, running, flying, and climbing. In order to receive a well-rounded education, all animal students took all subjects.

Across the board, the ducks excelled in swimming; in fact, some were truly gifted. But most of the ducks made only passing grades in flying, and all were very poor in running. To compensate, the ducks stayed after school for remedial running practice. After a few months, the ducks were so tired that soon they were only average in swimming, but average was acceptable in this school, so that was fine.

The rabbits started at the top of the class in running, but they were very poor swimmers. Also, the rabbits insisted on hopping around, and the teachers were concerned about their hyperactivity—so they made the rabbits walk everywhere instead of allowing them to run. Some were diagnosed with ADHD and put on Ritalin, and all of them had to come in early for special swimming classes.

The squirrels were excellent in climbing and running; in fact, when tasked with climbing a tree, they were the very best students. But the squirrels had trouble in the flying class. They wanted to first climb the tree, then spread their paws, and finally glide to the ground. (After all, that's the way squirrels fly.) But their teacher made them start on the ground instead of at the treetop, and the squirrels were not mastering the course material. So, every day a flying therapist took the squirrels into the gym and made them do front-paw exercises to strengthen their muscles so they could learn to fly the right way. This proved to be so taxing that some of the squirrels ultimately failed climbing.

The eagles were a constant problem. In climbing class, they beat all the others to the top of the tree, but they insisted on doing it their own way (which, naturally, involved flying). The eagles argued that it was the goal, not the method, that mattered, and because they were quite stubborn about this, the school psychologist diagnosed them as having oppositional-defiant disorder.

The obvious moral to the story is that we should be working *on*, not *in* our areas of weakness.

The 8 Most Common People Myths

When you think of how you could be more effective in life, where does your mind go first: working on improving your strengths or fixing your weaknesses? If you're like most people, you want to focus on your weaknesses first. However, I've never yet worked with someone who succeeded because they had a well-honed set of strong weaknesses. This may seem obvious, but considering how many people myths have become conventional wisdom, I'm going to take some time to debunk the most common of them, one by one:

1. People's basic weaknesses will change if they're coached.
2. The point of coaching is to help people manage their weaknesses.
3. Coaching will change the behavior of stubborn, poor performers.
4. Tough conversations damage relationships.
5. Being successful is about making sweeping life changes.
6. All age groups are motivated in the same way.
7. The person with the best qualifications wins.
8. When someone's personal life is in tatters, it doesn't necessarily affect his work.

1. Myth: People's Basic Weaknesses Will Change if They're Coached

Leopards don't change their spots. People should be coached and mentored, but you need to recognize that the best-case scenario for any employee is that he will become a better version of who he already is.

Though a wise person learns and develops skills and talents throughout the course of his life, his basic temperament won't change much. He'll have the same basic strengths and weaknesses at 50 that he had at 20.

If you like the basic package of who your employee is now, know that he will only get better in the future when you help him with coaching and training. However, if you *don't* like the basic package of who he is today, you're not going to turn him into a different person once you've spent all that development time, effort, and money on him. As the old English proverb says, "What's bred in the bone comes out in the flesh."

2. Myth: The Point of Coaching Is to Help People Manage Their Weaknesses

Everyone has weaknesses, including your star employees. Although it's true that her weaknesses will kill her if she can't tame them to some degree, the focus of coaching should be to capitalize on a person's strengths, not manage her weaknesses. When I'm coaching a person and we're discussing weaknesses, I'm hoping for four main outcomes:

1. **That he will increase his self-awareness.** Not many of us have a high degree of self-awareness. People are often unaware of how their areas of weakness affects others. My first goal is to help them see how others perceive them so they understand what they're best at, and what collateral damage is caused by refusing to work on controlling their areas of weakness.

2. **That she will own her areas of weakness and confess them to her team.** I'm a big believer in sharing areas of weakness with your colleagues— not to inform them of what they are (believe me, they already know), but to let them know that *you* know. People can forgive you for your weaknesses if they know you're aware of them and are at least trying to get better. But if you don't even know what they are, people laugh behind your back. As my brother says, "The difference between a sage and a fool is self-awareness."

3. **That he will adjust his role so that he can take advantage of his greatest strengths.** When coaching someone, I don't expect him to change the basic construct of who he is, because I don't believe that sort of change is sustainable over time. Neither is controlling weakness a winning strategy. You win by finding out your unique talents and gifts, and using them for most of your workday. As to your weaknesses, a better strategy is to get so amazing at what

you're already good at that people will *forgive* you for your weaknesses.

4. **That her newfound self-awareness will lead to some changes in her behavior.** She needs to focus on her strengths. I don't necessarily mean tasks that she's good at—we're all good at some things that drain and exhaust us— but finding those tasks that make her feel alive and excited, and give her energy, areas in which she can achieve more than anyone around her, because she was born to do those things. Once she identifies her natural talents, focuses on them, and builds skills around them, she will achieve far more than she ever thought she could.

3. Myth: Coaching Will Change the Behavior of Stubborn, Poor Performers

When was the last time you tried to make a grownup try to do something that she didn't want to do? It doesn't work. Unless she wants to do the task you're asking her to do, you're wasting your time.

A good test of your poor performer is to mention the possibility of receiving coaching. If her ears perk up and she expresses interest, maybe there's hope. If she doesn't seem enthusiastic about it, don't waste your time with elaborate, ongoing coaching efforts that go beyond the basics.

4. Myth: Tough Conversations Damage Relationships

Ironically, more often than not, just the reverse is true. When there's an elephant in the room and you have the courage to address it with kindness, it very rarely turns out as badly as you think it will. In fact, the great majority of tough conversations I've had have resulted in very positive outcomes.

Star leaders are able to have difficult conversations without making enemies. They earn respect and loyalty because they're willing to tackle these issues. They also approach tough talks from a place of care, not judgment, wanting to make the situation better for everyone.

One of my favorite CEOs had an employee who didn't show up for work. He missed a full day, then two, then three, and finally the entire week. He didn't call (or email or text) to say where he was. He also didn't respond to any communication.

The following week he came in and told my friend he had attempted suicide. My friend, the CEO, listened to him with a lot of sympathy and understanding. He advised the employee that the company was going to stand by him through this difficult time and would pay for him to see a counselor. He said the employee could take off any time that he needed to get back to health.

Then my friend changed direction, telling the employee that he (my friend) was going to "put on his boss hat," and informed the employee that he would be giving him a written warning that would appear on his employment record for skipping a week of work without any notice. He was incredulous. So my friend asked, "How do you think your absence affected your colleagues and customers?" The employee hadn't given it any thought, so my friend informed him that deadlines were missed, customers were inconvenienced and shorted, some of his coworkers had to work late, and everyone in his department was put under a lot of stress. The employee saw the truth in this, and accepted both the care and the reprimand.

Several years later this CEO assembled the staff to announce that he was leaving. The man who had attempted suicide was teary-eyed because he knew that the CEO cared personally about him, and was also willing to have the tough conversations necessary to make the business run properly.

I don't relate this story to recommend this as your course of action in a similar situation, but to illustrate the fact that difficult conversations can turn out well if they come from a place of respect and trust.

5. Myth: Being Successful Is About Making Sweeping Life Changes

Typically, sweeping changes are short-lived. Real change happens more gradually and takes more enduring effort. Each day is a choice to keep putting one foot in front of the other, and stay running in the right direction.

A successful coaching engagement is more like a marathon than a sprint. At the beginning of a marathon, participants are excited and enthusiastic about running. They feel fresh, they're rested, and they've trained for months. A new day is dawning, and tremendous energy from spectators and other runners surrounds them. The situation changes, though, when they're into the third hour of the race. There isn't any cheering, the pack has thinned out, and they feel alone. Those who complete the race are the ones who keep on running at mile 19, even though it's hard.

Here's the encouraging news for anyone who's trying to make a life change: If you get 1 percent better every three days, in seven months you'll be twice as good as you are today. If that feels too difficult, maybe you can get 1 percent better each week. At that rate, you'll be twice as good as you are today in about a year and a half. It doesn't take a super achiever to do that. All it takes is someone committed to getting a little bit better each day and to finishing the race.

It is also worth noting that we typically overestimate what we can accomplish in six months, but underestimate what we can accomplish in three years.

6. Myth: All Age Groups Are Motivated in the Same Way

Members of different generations tend to view the workplace differently and tend to be motivated by different things. If you use the same approach with everyone, you'll be missing the mark. Here is a general view of loyalties at work by generation:

Generation	Born	Loyal To
Traditionalists	1925–1945	The company
Baby Boomers	1946–1964	Their own advancement (career, money, and promotions)
Generation Xers	1965–1985	Their manager
Millennials	1986–1999	Their coworkers—not to the organization, not to their manager, but to their friends
Generation Zers	2000–2017	People who take the initiative to build relationship with them

Maybe you belong to one of these generations and don't value any of these things. I realize this chart paints with a pretty broad brush, but it is a helpful guide to working with different generations.

TRADITIONALISTS

Traditionalists are mostly absent from the workplace today. They still occupy board seats and retain ownership positions, but they occupy fewer and fewer operational seats as the years go by.

They were very dedicated workers; they won World War II, and built the country and many companies that we work for today. If you don't care about the country or the company, they don't have a lot of time for you.

Baby Boomers

Baby Boomers still dominate the workplace, and they tend to care very much about advancing and achieving. They are the generation that remade our culture. They embraced the sexual revolution and rock and roll, and rewrote the social contract in North America.

In the workplace, they have no intention of merely advancing the company's interests. They want to achieve, and to receive the money and status that achievement brings. As a result, they're willing to make sacrifices for their career without giving the matter too much thought. They believe in progress and like the language of achievement.

Generation Xers

Generation Xers lived through the fall of the Soviet Union, survived disco (barely, in my case—it nearly slayed me), and embraced the need for change in the world. They like justice and social causes. They witnessed the public disgrace of leaders in almost every major sector of society— such as the political scandals of Richard Nixon and Bill Clinton, the public fall of the televangelists and the abuse scandals of the Catholic Church, the tainted blood scandals of the Red Cross, scandals in the military, and corporate criminality symbolized by the bankruptcy of Enron.

Generation Xers are cynical about leaders in general, and so tend to place a lot of trust in their immediate manager, whom they know personally. The manager holds the key to their salary, working conditions, and promotions, and they will often follow a manager from workplace to workplace.

Millennials

Millennials may be educated, socially conscious, liberal in their thinking, family-focused, and interested in lifestyle and experiences. They care a lot about having opportunities to build friendships at work and developing strong relationships with their coworkers.

When working with Millennials, you need to care about building a positive culture that treats everyone fairly and well; this is what they value and require to be happy and productive. They tend to side with each other, not necessarily with you or with the company. Use that to your advantage by making team-based incentives and rewards. Communicate well and often so that they feel cared-for and included.

Generation Zers

Sometimes called "Post-Millennials," Generation Zers have grown up immersed in the internet and technology. Whereas older generations view technology as a tool, for Generation Z, it's the water they swim in. It's how they shop, socialize with each other, entertain themselves, and learn about the world. They've lived their lives in the shadow of terrorist threats, and have been shaped by the "great recession." They have no memory of a time when these factors were not an issue in the world.

They show early signs of being a responsible generation, with lower teen pregnancy rates, less substance abuse, and higher graduation rates.

In his 1982 bestseller, *Megatrends,* John Naisbitt first developed the idea of "high tech, high touch." He believed that in a world of technology, people would long for personal, human interaction. It's one of the few predictions from futurists of that time that have proven to be true, no more so in the case of Generation Z. Because of their extreme internet dependence, I believe they have a hunger for human contact. They need older, wiser, caring people to speak into their lives. They want a work environment that provides stability, unlike the unstable world they've grown up in. Mentor your Gen Zers. Give them feedback. Shape them into a team in which they can find a place to relate, contribute, and belong.

7. Myth: The Person With the Best Qualifications Wins

Qualifications *alone* don't guarantee that a person is going to be a fit for your company. This truth is borne out by the fact that I've made some unlikely hiring recommendations that turned out really well. How about an academic serving in the president's office of a university, never having sold anything in his life, being hired as a sales team leader? Or a career leader of a millwork business moving over to run an agriculture company with a global marketplace?

These hires might not make sense at first glance, but these unlikely moves were successful because the academic was bright, people-savvy, and eager to learn and grow; and the millwork manager was a natural-born leader with incredible drive, vision, and a keen eye for quality. Though they didn't precisely "qualify" for the jobs on paper, they had all the right "fit" characteristics. They both shared values with the companies that they transitioned to. All they had to learn was how the new businesses ran. Within a year, both were at full gallop.

Skill is needed, but if you have to weigh skill against fit, choose fit every time.

8. Myth: When Someone's Personal Life Is in Tatters, It Doesn't Necessarily Affect His Work

I don't believe this to be true. Although we all go through hard times personally and keep things together at work in the meantime, we're also deeply affected by what's going on at home. At the end of the day, your personal and professional lives are the same life. If your work life is going badly, your loved ones feel it at home. If your home life is in turmoil, people often feel it at work.

It's not your job as a coach to help people fix their home lives. It's your job to help them understand that what's going on at home can affect their coworkers, and to learn and manage this important principle: leave your personal life at the door. This means that when an employee enters the door of the work site, she does her best to shake off what's happening at home. Coworkers shouldn't feel compelled to be counselors, nor should they endure poor treatment because things at home are tough.

Bad behavior that spills over from personal to work life needs to be addressed.

People Action Steps

- Sit with each of your direct reports, help them identify their greatest strengths, and brainstorm with them about how they can capitalize on those strengths in their roles.
- Stop pouring time into people who aren't interested in growing. Instead, focus your time on coaching and developing those who are eager to move ahead.
- Develop your team's self-awareness by having them identify their own greatest areas of strength and challenge in a group setting. Lead the way by going first and being very honest. Laugh. Make it okay to have both.
- Help each of your direct reports set one small, achievable goal that takes advantage of their strengths and provides something they can focus on for the next three months.

In Summary

- Leopards don't change their spots, and the person that you are coaching will one day be just a better version of who he already is.

- You should coach people primarily to build on areas of strength, not just control areas of weakness.
- You can never make a grown-up do something she doesn't want to do.
- Tough conversations from a caring boss strengthen, not weaken, the relationship.
- Getting 1 percent better every week through consistent coaching means that you'll be twice as good as you are today in about a year and a half.
- Each generation is motivated differently, and a wise coach treats them accordingly.
- Hire for fit; train for skill.
- Though a person's personal and professional life are the same life, a professional will do his best to separate the two, and not over-burden coworkers.

7

Identify Problems That Might Cause Your Stars to Leave

"If I have to chase and fight for your attention, eventually I won't want it anymore."

—Will Smith, American actor, producer, rapper, and songwriter

I've worked with hundreds of stars, and you need to know one thing up-front. Someone right now is sitting in a boardroom somewhere trying to devise a plan to poach them from you. That's typically *how* stars end up leaving: they're poached by someone who appreciates them more than you do—someone who offers them a new challenge and/or a better work environment.

Everyone who interacts with your stars—all of your competitors, suppliers, and customers, for a start, plus all the people they meet at trade shows and the people who interact with them socially—sees them for what they are. There's danger everywhere! I can't count the number of people who have been recruited by a savvy owner or CEO while having a casual conversation at some social event or work-related function.

It may surprise you to learn that stars typically don't leave over money. Now, I'll insert a caveat that if it's *crazy* money, all bets are off. But even then, stars think long and hard, and feel very conflicted about leaving for bigger money if they're happy with the other parts of their current job.

A client of mine had a very senior manager who was respected throughout his industry and had a lot of autonomy. He was actively recruited by a non-competing company in the same industry that finally offered him nearly *double* his current salary. The manager struggled to make a decision, because, apart from the money, he felt that the actual *job* he was being offered was more challenging and better suited to his talents than his current one. Still, he came to management with the offer in hand, asking them if they could come anywhere close to matching it. They couldn't, and he reluctantly decided to leave. However, he gave three months' notice and insisted to his new company that he stay on with his current employer for six months in a consulting capacity. It took a lot of money, an excellent opportunity, and a lot of concessions for this star to leave his job.

The Top-3 Reasons Stars Leave a Company

Stars *do* leave over money when monetary compensation is really just a symptom of a bigger problem. But if a star is fairly paid relative to others in the industry, money isn't generally the biggest issue. Here are the top three issues that cause a Star to leave:

1. Being forced to work with non-stars.
2. Being forced to report to a non-star.
3. Feeling bored and under-challenged.

1. Being Forced to Work With Non-Stars

If your stars work in an environment in which they're forced to interact on a consistent basis with coworkers who are non-stars, you should be worried, because they *are* a flight risk. Eventually, they're going to go somewhere that's more serious about taking action with the Star Chart.

On this point, a CEO friend of mine once gave me an object lesson. He held out both hands, palms down and fists closed. Then he said, "Imagine that you have two team members, one in each hand. One is an 'A' player, and the other is a 'C' player. Now, pick which one you want to keep, because you can't have both. If you choose to keep your 'C' player, then you're also choosing to let go of your 'A' player, because he won't work with the 'C' player."

Which one do *you* want to keep? Because remember: you can't have both.

After reading a lot about The Container Store—which for 14 years in a row has won *Fortune* magazine's Best Place to Work in America Award—I took a trip to visit the store nearest to my home. While there I spoke with the manager and several employees, and a clear and consistent theme emerged. To paraphrase one employee, "Everywhere else

I've worked, I've always been the hardest worker, and I've been forced to work with people who don't care and who make the same money. I couldn't stand it. At The Container Store, we all care, we get a lot of training, and we all work hard or we wouldn't be allowed to stay, so I love coming to work. I don't work with any slackers here, not a single one. Everyone who works here is passionate about what we do."

The manager told me that people were so excited about working in this environment that they had a huge surplus of qualified applicants, and were able to choose only the best; people who were already raving fans.

Stars want to work with other stars.

2. Being Forced to Report to a Non-Star

They key to happiness (or misery) for any employee is the quality of the relationship that she has with her direct supervisor. This is actually more important than the caliber of the company. An employee working for a star in a weak company can be very happy. An employee working for a non-star in a great company will never be happy—and won't stay, either, no matter how amazing or famous the company is.

The simple fact is that employees join companies and leave managers. If an employee's direct supervisor cares about her, knows her priorities and career goals, and acts as a career advocate for her, she will be happy and will stick around. However, if an employee feels that her supervisor is incompetent or doesn't live out the company's right attitudes, or doesn't like her personally, she'll be primed for flight. In this scenario, it's the stars who leave first, because stars can easily find other places to work.

When a non-star is allowed into a leadership role, the stars working under him are at immediate flight risk. This is called "dumbsizing," because it's the same as deliberately cutting your best players. The only people who will tolerate reporting to a non-star are those who don't have any other options—your other non-stars. Dumbsizing is the downsizing of a department by losing all your best players and keeping all your worst ones.

Your stars have all the options in the world, and if they're forced into this sort of a reporting relationship, they won't be around for long. They'll give the company a little bit of time to see if leaders recognize their mistake, but if they perceive that the company is set on enforcing this injustice over the long term, they will leave.

3. Feeling Bored and Under-Challenged

When a star feels that she has stopped growing and is getting stale, and sees no way for that to change, she often thinks about moving on. After all, that's a good reason to leave, isn't it?! Wrong fits and productive-but-difficults are happy to "quit and stay," but stars don't think like that. They want to grow!

The interesting thing is, many times I've seen stars leave for a place that offers *less* money, because the new place is a better values fit, or offers more challenge and/or opportunity. Consider the following story about a star leader—the general manager of a large, flagship location at a fashionable, high-paying, high-profile restaurant—who was recruited by a smaller entrepreneurial company with lots of enthusiasm, but not a lot of internal systems.

One day I sat with this young leader and asked him why he made the switch. First, he talked about boredom: *"I'd worked for the company for years, and I just didn't see any more challenge on the horizon. I'd gone as far as I could go with them. I didn't think I'd ever be considered for a senior position in the company. Leadership had me pegged as a location manager, and since my results were good, I knew that wasn't going to change for a long time."*

The second part of his answer was about feeling ignored: *"As I looked at the overall business, I could see lots of things that needed to be improved. I kept a running list, but the company rep who oversaw my store wasn't interested in hearing about it. He only wanted to see my numbers grow week over week. He didn't care what my career goals were, or about how I could develop further. He really didn't care about me as person. In the past, I had talked directly with the owners of the business and had some creative input in the direction of the company, but now I only talked to this corporate drone. I was fed up with it."*

This star ended up taking a lower salary with my client because he liked the people, appreciated their values, and believed that he could contribute to the growth of the business. ***He could matter again.***

Stars aren't recruited; they're attracted—and they're attracted to opportunity.

Stars want to play on a team with other stars. They want an opportunity to prove that they *are* stars, and they want to grow. The more serious you get about taking action around the Star Chart, the more stars you will attract—and the more stars you attract, the easier it will be to attract even more. That's why the best teams gather more and more momentum: because people everywhere are attracted to being with great people in places that are growing.

Learning to Allocate Your Time Wisely

And now it is time to take a good, hard look at *yourself.* Are you doing everything you can to retain your stars? Start by asking where you focus. Is the majority of your time spent with your stars, developing, coaching, and encouraging them to be even better? Are you thinking through strategies to retain them, so that when they get other offers (which they will) they'll choose to stay with you?

Or is the bulk of your time spent pouring your energy into your non-stars (your wrong fits and productive-but-difficults)? Non-stars take a lot of time and mental energy. They occupy your mind at work, and you worry about them when you're at home. Most leaders spend the bulk of their time working with the whiners, not the winners. Think about the difference between the two:

Winners	**Whiners**
Take responsibility for their actions	Are victims of circumstance or other people
Brighten a room by entering it	Brighten a room by leaving it
Build strong relationships	Destroy relationships
Work independently	Need your help
Get things done	Make excuses
View life as an exciting adventure	View life is an ordeal to get through
Free up your time	Suck your time

The people you surround yourself with either raise your game or lower it. This is true in your personal life, with the friends you choose, and it's true in your professional life, too. Every member of your team needs to lift the average, because no one succeeds alone. Every day, winners remind us by their actions how to show our best selves to the world and how to become better and better at what we do.

People Action Steps

- Conduct exit interviews with Stars who leave to find out why they're going. Make sure it isn't because they're working with or reporting to a non-star.
- Make sure your non-stars never get into a position of leadership, because they will put your company in danger of losing its best people.

- When you're looking to fill a key role, ask your stars for referrals. Birds of a feather flock together.

In Summary

Stars leave for three main reasons:

1. Being forced to work with non-stars.
2. Being forced to report to a non-star. This is much worse than just working with one. People join companies and leave managers.
3. Feeling bored and under-challenged. Make sure your stars have lots of runway in front of them so they can grow.

Stars aren't attracted, they're recruited to growing companies made up of great people. The best want to work with the best. Use your time wisely by investing and developing your best people to become better and better at what they're already good at.

8

Reward and Develop Your Stars (The "A Box")

"People work for money but go the extra mile for praise, recognition, and rewards."

—Dale Carnegie, leadership training guru and author of *How to Win Friends and Influence People*

Back in the salad days when I was a freshly hatched sales person, I sat through a training course where they taught us about the "Silver Platter Syndrome." The idea was that, while you were spending the bulk of your time on your problem customers (who you wished you didn't have), your best accounts were being serviced up on a silver platter for your competitors to pick off because you were (unintentionally) ignoring them. Silver Platter Syndrome works precisely the same way with your stars.

The harsh reality is that while you spend your time with your whiners, your winners are being served up on a platter for someone else who will show them more attention and appreciation.

It's easy to ignore your stars because they don't require a lot of attention. They just go about their day getting things done. But ignore them at your peril—because right now someone is plotting to steal your stars. Maybe it's a customer, a supplier, or a competitor. Maybe it's someone your stars know socially or someone they met at a trade show.

What's your plan to hold onto your stars when they're tempted with a better offer?

Make sure your stars feel appreciated. Give them rewards—lots of rewards. And give them the independence they need to do a great job, and the support they desire to get better and better at what they do.

Holding Onto Your Stars

As leaders, when we review our people, we naturally tend to focus on problem areas and how to fix them, and our HR plans reflect that. We know we need to talk to this person about their bad behavior or deal with that icky situation somehow. These sorts of plans are always on our minds. But what about your stars? Do you have a plan for retaining and developing them? Tending to your stars is the single most important task you have as leader. Luckily, the HR plan for stars is quite simple—and fun to execute. In brief, you want to:

- Show them love.
- Give them perks.
- Challenge them.
- Give them opportunities to grow.

When you customize your efforts and do this well, it's exhilarating to watch your stars thrive. You might start with these top-10 rewards.

The 10 Most Persuasive Rewards

You retain stars by giving them love. Love can look like a lot of things, depending on the person. These may include:

1. Money.
2. Personalized gifts.
3. Recognition.
4. Personal growth.
5. Status.
6. Autonomy.
7. Insider access.
8. Personal attention.
9. Perks.
10. Increased responsibility.

1. Money

Money matters. Your stars need to be paid at the highest level of what constitutes fair-market compensation in your industry. However, I've found that money matters almost as much for the recognition it brings as it does for the increased cash the star has in her hands.

If you're going to offer a raise, bonus, or incentive plan to someone, offer it to the person who is actively building your business, not the person who is nesting in it. You're not running a daycare.

Build a culture that values merit and contribution, not seniority. Often I find that 20 years of experience is actually five years of experience repeated four times over. The person has been in the role for a long time, but she hasn't grown or added new skills that warrant higher compensation. Her years of experience don't necessarily reflect the level of skill she brings to the job. Low turnover isn't necessarily a strength. Often it just means that important issues never get addressed.

Ironically, too much money can be a disincentive, too. If compensation levels are so rich that there's nothing left to strive for, they're probably too high. Compensation for stars should be high *relative to your industry*, which means different things for different companies. This said, make sure that your stars are fairly paid and that money is never a reason for them to look elsewhere.

2. Personalized Gifts

Sometimes a timely gift means more than a raise and has the advantage of adding memory value. Even simple gifts mean a lot when they're sincerely given. Flowers, books, gift certificates, chocolates, mementoes, and so on that are accompanied with a card containing meaningful words never go wrong. Likewise, an extravagant gift that is sincerely given will work magic—especially if it becomes a memento and a talking point for the recipient.

Back in the day, I worked as a sales rep for a large company. At my first trade show, I determined that I was going to put in a serious effort and distinguish myself on the team. I called clients to meet me at the booth before the show started. I helped with setup and tear-down. I made sure my breaks were short, and engaged every prospect, assuming they would buy. I never gave in to the temptation of sitting back and giving out brochures. I even took off my watch so that I wouldn't look at it during slow times.

The show was a success, and when we came home, my boss presented me with a large—no, huge—antique humidor built of Spanish cedar, fronted with a glass door, and stocked with expensive Cuban cigars. As humidors go, it was spectacular—as were his kind words when he presented the gift to me publicly, during a sales meeting. He even had a plaque installed on the back engraved with some compliments about my performance and the dates of the show.

It was a beautiful piece of furniture and a fairly costly gift. I was touched and impressed. Had he given me $1,000 in cash, I would've put new tires on my car and taken my wife out to dinner, and it would be long forgotten.

Twenty years later, the humidor still sits in my office; in fact, I'm looking at it right now as I type these words. It's simply the best humidor I've ever heard of, let alone seen. It even has most of the original cigars still in it, because, as luck would have it, I don't smoke. That minor detail aside, visitors to my office often comment on it, and, even though years have passed, it still reminds me of that experience.

3. Recognition

Most leaders are reluctant to give praise, and that's a big mistake. When praise is deserved, a leader is presented with a great opportunity to motivate and to reinforce right attitudes with the entire team.

Publicly and privately praise people who live out your right attitudes. Write them notes; give them awards. Recognition doesn't have to cost anything. It's not about the money, it's about being noticed for what you do.

Recognition means most when it's both deserved and unexpected. If someone gets chosen as Employee of the Month every month, and everyone knows that eventually they will get their turn on the recognition board, it doesn't mean a whole lot. But an unexpected shout-out during a staff meeting that tells your employee someone is noticing when he does things right means a great deal.

My daughter worked at a fast-food restaurant as a teenager, and the day she was publicly recognized and awarded the status of being a Key Holder was an important day for her. She shared it with the family with pride over dinner. It showed that she was trusted and moving forward in her job.

4. Personal Growth

For the employee, this includes attending events or conferences, engaging in external coaching, gaining access to webinars, receiving funded educational opportunities, and obtaining book allowances. It means a lot to an employee to be selected to attend an industry conference or fly to another city to learn a new skill.

Personal growth opportunities are particularly gratifying for your stars because they confirm their status internally with coworkers ("Susie gets to go where?") and gives them bragging rights at home ("Yes, I'm off to Los Angeles on Monday for a conference."). These opportunities benefit the employee with more knowledge and contacts, and also benefit the company when the employee brings her new skills back to the workplace. If she gives a formal summary to her colleagues when she gets back, the benefits extend even further. It's a win for everyone.

5. Status

Think better titles, nicer office space, bigger expense accounts, better hours, nicer parking access, and more important responsibilities. Many people are motivated by some combination of these four things:

1. Status.
2. Money.
3. Power.
4. Popularity.

Though these categories don't always reflect our inner Albert Schweitzer, and recognizing that there's a potential evil side to each of them, there is a lot of truth to the list. It should be known in your company that people who work harder get more of the currency they want.

6. Autonomy

There was a time when the American military had no use for independent thinkers. That changed in World War II, and General George Patton played a big part in the change. He wrote, "Never tell people how to do things. Tell them what you want done and they will surprise you with their ingenuity."[1]

David Petraeus, the four-star general who commanded coalition forces in Iraq, had the same philosophy, looking for leaders who "were flexible and able to think independently."[2] While he was in command, violence plummeted.

William Coyne, senior vice president of research and development at the famously innovative 3M, described it this way: "We let our people know what we want them to accomplish. But—and it is a very big but—we do not tell them how to achieve those goals."[3]

As much as possible, let your stars figure things out on their own. Autonomy is prized by everyone, but stars value it most, and make the best use of it. I'm a firm believer in the maxim "don't harness a racehorse." A harness only holds a racehorse back—it may even be an irritation.

Autonomy is about letting people have control of:

- Their own to-do lists—prioritizing what needs to be done by when.
- Their own methods—figuring out the best way to get the work done.

- Their own work hours—having the ability to work remotely, or having some flexibility in their schedule.

Some of these will work for your company and some won't. Choose the version of autonomy that works for you and let your stars surprise you with their ingenuity.

7. Insider Access

One of the great motivators of human nature is the drive to be included in the inner circle. We all understand this because we've been through grade school. Kids will throw away their morals, their inhibitions, and sometimes their self-respect to be an insider. They'll turn on close friends, lie to their families, throw away their education, ruin their health, and endure punishment from authorities, just as long as they have access to the inner circle that matters to them. This doesn't change once we've grown up; everyone in your company wants desperately to feel that they have access to the inner circle.

Rather than fight this reality, give your stars inner-circle access as a reward. Invite them to attend part of a management meeting or retreat. Call them into your office or ask them to lunch and solicit their opinion on an important strategic decision. Arrange for them to spend time with key leaders in the company.

Award your stars access to the inner circle, even if it isn't permanent. Access matters to them. A lot.

8. Personal Attention

I've interviewed many stars who were looking at a new position because they felt ignored by top management. Sometimes we think we can forget about these people because they always figure things out on their own, and we turn our attention elsewhere.

Stars feel it and don't like it. They want to know that they're on your radar, that you know their plans and goals, and that you are acting as their career advocate. The biggest mistake you can make with your star is to ignore him, setting him up to be noticed by someone else. In our personal lives, we need to remember to keep the home fires burning, and the same is true at work. Don't ignore the ones you love the most.

9. Perks

Some airlines have figured out that—at least in some respects—loyalty can be bought in exchange for perks. Do you know anyone who buys things he doesn't need or takes an extra flight so he can retain his ultra-triple-platinum frequent-flyer status so he doesn't have to board alongside the unwashed masses or sit in steerage with the rest of the hoi polloi? Perks have the power to retain people.

Perks can take many forms such as time off, upgraded technology, or enhanced travel status. I have clients who regularly offer new phones and laptops as rewards. One client allows stars to upgrade flights to business class or have access to airport VIP lounges. Another collects "swag" (gifts given to them by suppliers), and gives them out as prizes to stars. One restaurant chain allows free food for people who hit their goals.

Find perks that matter to your stars and trade them for retention.

10. Increased Responsibility

More work is a reward? Really?!

While non-stars are unhappy with more work, stars love knowing that they have your confidence. More responsibility is often a perk to them, especially when the increased responsibility is noticed by others. Giving your star a chance to be the boss while you are on a vacation or lead a team huddle in your absence lets him try out his leadership skills, and also lets him know that he's trusted and valued.

Hold on to your stars. Here's the HR recipe:

- Show them love.
- Give them perks.
- Challenge them.
- Give them opportunities to grow.

People Action Steps

- Make a list of your stars and ask yourself what growth opportunities you're offering to keep them interested this year.

- Sit with each of your stars individually, and ask what their career goals are and how you can facilitate their achievement.
- Keep a list of people who you've praised or recognized and the date you did it. Review it monthly.
- Invite a growing leader to a core inner leadership circle meeting to give her a taste of the inner circle.
- Ask a bright younger person his advice about a weighty strategic question the business is facing.

In Summary

There are several ways to reward your stars. These include:

- Making sure they're paid at the top of their wage scale.
- Giving them personalized gifts that go beyond cash, to cement great memories in their minds.
- Recognizing them in public and private for a job well done.
- Offering opportunities for personal growth like book allowances and educational seminars.
- Giving out status symbols such as fancier titles, better offices, and nicer parking access.

- Trusting them with the autonomy to make their own decisions and have flexibility with their work hours.
- Securing access to the inner circle, which gives them a taste of leadership, even if the access isn't permanent.
- Providing personal attention so they don't feel forgotten.
- Rewarding them with perks including time off, upgraded technology, travel arrangements, and company "swag."
- Offering increased responsibility that tells them they're trusted with important responsibilities.

Use one or more of these tools to make sure your stars are happy and disinclined to look elsewhere.

9

Coach Your Potential Stars
(The "B Box")

"Potential just means you haven't done it yet."

—Variously attributed

We have all been in the potential star box of the Star Chart, particularly when starting our careers or beginning a new job. Sometimes potential stars are just young or new to the position. A 16-year-old may share all of your right attitudes, but needs to mature before he becomes more productive. Or, you may have made a new and great hire, but she isn't going to be terribly productive until she has completed one business cycle with you and gained experience. This problem will largely take care of itself.

Though we have all temporarily occupied the potential star box at various points in our careers, it isn't a box that's meant to be lived in. It's the box we want our employees to pass through on their way to the star box.

As you recall from Chapter 5, folks who land in the potential star box score high on the right attitude axis but low on the effectiveness axis. Typically, two kinds of people land in this box: those who aren't productive because they're still learning, and those who have settled in for a long winter's nap with less-than-great performance on a more-or-less permanent basis. The still-learning group is easy to deal with, because they aren't in the box for very long; they're just passing through. Those who want to nest in this box are tougher, and they will be the main focus of this chapter.

6 Telltale Signs of Someone Who's Nesting in the Potential Star Box

You can easily identify potential stars, because, for the most part, you like them. The reason that they are still around, in fact, is that they're likeable, despite their lack of productivity. Sometimes people in this box of the Star Chart aren't good enough to rehire, but aren't bad enough to fire, either. You feel "on the bubble" about them.

Potential stars have at least some of the right attitudes that are important to you. They may qualify for this box by a whisker, but they're not hard on you or the organization. They aren't terrible; they certainly aren't great either. You find yourself feeling unsatisfied with their performance, and wishing they would "step it up" and be more productive. In most companies, they stay around for a long time and their under-performance is never addressed.

Here are the top indicators that someone fits into this Star Chart box:

1. He Doesn't Show Passion for His Work

Though he may enjoy his work on some level and even complete it in a mostly satisfactory way, it's obvious to others that he doesn't have a lot of passion. He may even openly admit this to coworkers, talking at length about what his true passion is. If he had the choice, he'd stay home every day instead of go to work. These folks make a lifestyle out of "working for the weekend."

Obviously, this type of employee doesn't score a 10 on the "right attitudes" axis, but he might score a six, which still puts him in the potential star box.

2. She Doesn't Show Much Interest in Improving

She may not be content with her level of pay or her work conditions, but she *is* content with the contribution she's making. She isn't interested in going to seminars (unless it means a day away from work or going on a fun trip), taking courses, or reading books on how she can get better at her job, particularly if it requires any time commitment beyond her regular work hours.

In short, she's not interested in becoming a master at what she does. She would rather maintain the status quo, and doesn't love seeing the boat rocked. Again, she is too good to fire, but not quite good enough to rehire, either.

3. He Needs Support From Others to Accomplish His Basic Duties

He may be willing—even eager—to learn, but at the end of the day, he needs help and support from his colleagues to get the job done. Your heart may sink as you see him approaching, full of cheeriness and incompetence, asking for something from you yet again. He may remind you of the kid in middle school who just kept putting his hand up to say, "Teacher, I don't get it." When she said, "What don't you get?" He would respond with, "I don't know. I just don't get it." And it never got better; he never got it.

Many potential stars don't seem to grow in their confidence or ability over time, and this actually may not be their fault. It could be that they've been promoted beyond their abilities, aren't suited to the job, or don't have the aptitude for it.

4. She Protects Her Job by Hoarding Information

She may feel insecure about her standing in the company for a variety of reasons. Maybe she notices the lack of standing ovations coming from her boss. Maybe she knows her performance isn't as good as other people's.

In the worst-case scenario, this can lead to information hoarding or turf wars (fighting for something other than the good of the company). Hoarders believe that they're more secure if all of the information relevant to their job remains as their own "tribal knowledge"; in other words, it stays in their head, doesn't get put on paper, and certainly doesn't get taught to anyone else. Any suggestion of doing these things (which, by the way, would safeguard the company, because none of us can *guarantee* we'll be able to work another day) are seen as a threat to her power, and she resists them—sometimes with a quiet will of iron—but resists nonetheless.

They can be right about winning job security through information hoarding, but only if the leader allows themselves to be held hostage to this tactic.

If you've worried about an employee who is a bottleneck due to the vast amount of information that resides with her alone, and who is reluctant to share it, you know that you're likely dealing with someone from the potential star box. However, if this employee starts using information as a weapon, she belongs to a lower box. More on that to come.

5. He Measures Hours, Not Productivity

Somewhere along the way, the potential star has bought into the idea that it's about time spent, not outcomes accomplished. He may scramble to find hours to add to his tally, such as time spent commuting, waiting for airplanes, and sitting alone in hotel rooms, or untraceable and unverifiable hours "worked at home." In the absence of productivity, I remain agnostic about the reality of these sorts of claimed hours.

6. She Is Willing to Work Hard, Provided Her Incentives Increase

This is a particularly bad sign, because it indicates an entitlement mindset. Great people need to be well compensated, but it's clear that they're working for something other than money. Ironically, when money is a person's aim, she often doesn't end up with much of it.

The best businesspeople I know *do not* work for money. They work hard because they want to make a difference in someone's life, or because they have passion to implement an idea, or fix something that's broken. For many of them, money is an incidental that they certainly enjoy, but they view much it in the same way a pioneer farmer of the past viewed grain: it tasted great as a nice loaf of bread, but its main purpose was to be used as seed to plant larger fields for the next year.

When an employee is fairly paid, but still needs prodding and incentivizing to get her job done, it's a sign she's stuck in the potential star box.

Giving Potential Stars the Support They Need to Shine

As a young man, Clint worked for his father, who became very critical of his work performance. He decided that Clint was a B-boxer, and finally let him go. Clint was angry, and drifted through his dad's industry in a series of low-level jobs. He didn't really know what to do with his life, as he had always assumed that he would be his dad's successor.

As time went on and Clint gained experience outside the family business, he began to see his dad's business from a different perspective. He could see that change was coming to the industry overall, so he joined a large company that he believed was positioned to catch the wave of the future. He worked there for a few years, made some good friends, and one day left to found his own business.

Twenty-five years later, Clint is one of the leading players in his entire industry throughout North America. Many of his former bosses from his days at the large company work for him now. He has been featured in industry magazines and is looked up to as someone who really "gets it." Clint and his dad reconciled, and today his dad recognizes that his talented son was only passing through the potential star box.

Potential stars sometimes start *nesting* in the B box of the Star Chart. Take note of these nesters, as they require your intervention. Nesters never get better on their own, but they may improve if you take the time to help them move forward. Whether they're nesting or just passing through this box, the ideas that follow are the most effective strategies in your HR toolkit to prod and develop your potential star. The one non-negotiable with someone in this box of the Star Chart is that he or she must eventually move into the star box.

Train and/or Coach Them

You may have an employee who is a good personality fit for her role and is well liked by coworkers, but lacks the skills required for her job. In the Star Chart, she scores high on right attitudes, but low on effectiveness. If she had stronger computer skills or had a forklift ticket, or could read a profit and loss statement, or had deeper knowledge of the product, she could be a star. This is a comparatively easy fix. Help this employee get the training that she needs so she can move out of the potential star box and into the star box.

Discussions with potential stars should be friendly and earnest. If these people really do fit in this box, they want to move into a star box, and are upset to find that they aren't there already. These are good people. They share many of the attitudes that are important to you. They're worth your coaching efforts. Investing time in them can shape them into the successful contributors that they really do want to be.

Clarify Your Expectations

Many employees simply lack self-awareness. This is a very common problem, and it's not going to solve itself. Frequently people in the potential star box assume they are stars—that is, if they even reflect on their performance at all. This is actually one of the most common causes of people living and nesting permanently in the potential star box. In truth, no one has ever cared enough to have a reality conversation with them, telling them that they are living in a less-than-wonderful box and what, specifically, they need to do to get out of it.

A CEO once requested that I sit with a senior manager who was struggling in his role. I showed the employee the Star Chart and asked him where he would plot himself. He looked at it for a long time and, with tears in his eyes, confided to me that he felt sometimes that he was not a star, but only a potential star.

The CEO joined our discussion, and I asked him to outline specifically what changes would need to happen for him to consider this person a star performer. He listed three things that were all quite do-able. I asked the employee if he felt that he could accomplish these things, and he replied with an enthusiastic "yes." He had no idea that the CEO had these expectations for him, and was confident that he could achieve them, now that he knew what they were. Within a couple of months, and with the help of some job coaching, he had arrived in the star box. Several years later, that person was still in the star box and doing just fine.

Sometimes helping an employee gain a new sense of self-awareness and clarifying your expectations are all that are needed for him to get into the star box.

Change Their Role

A person can get stuck in the potential star box because she is in a role that isn't really a fit for her personality, skill set, or level of intelligence. When an employee shows up for work every day comparing her weakness to everyone else's strength, it's not terribly motivating. An extroverted people person that gets stuck in data entry is not going to be happy, and no matter how great her work ethic is, she is unlikely to move beyond the potential star box. In fact, it's much more likely that she'll bounce all over the bad regions of the Star Chart as her confidence and attitude erode.

A person who doesn't want to deal with people and conflict isn't going to be happy in a management role, no matter how great her attitude is and how much her values line up with the company's. It will take your specific intervention to help sort out her role and move her into a seat that will maximize her strengths.

I once worked with a CEO client who elevated a long-time star into a senior role. He had always shown a great attitude, was solidly productive, and was highly respected by his colleagues. Everyone was happy for him and felt that he deserved the promotion.

Things seemed to be going well for the first couple of months, but soon this person seemed to be drifting out of the star box and migrating through the other three boxes. It became impossible to know how he would show up on any given day. Some days he would come to work as a star, some days he seemed like a productive-but-difficult (which was not in character for him), and other times he seemed like an outright fireable wrong fit.

Finally, the CEO sat with him and had a serious heart-to-heart talk, and the employee said, "I used to love coming to work. I knew what to do in my role and I was good at it. Everyone liked me, and I really enjoyed my job. Now, I can't sleep because of all of the stress I'm under. People who used to be my friends look at me with suspicion. I feel overwhelmed by everything that has to get done, and I hate all of the conflict this job requires me to deal with."

After some negotiation, they agreed that he would step back into the role he had before taking the promotion. He instantly was back to being the star that he had been before the change, and everyone was happy.

Boost the performance of your potentials stars! Here's the recipe:

- Coach and train them.
- Clarify your expectations.
- Change their role.
- Have a reality conversation with them.

People Action Steps

- Decide whether your potential stars are en route to the star box, or have become permanently comfortable, nesting in the company as an underperformer.
- Assign each employee in the potential star box of the Star Chart five measurable accountabilities for the quarter, and review them in a group setting weekly to increase visibility and accountability.

In Summary

Two types of people typically occupy the potential star box: those who are there temporarily while en route to living permanently in the star box, and those who have begun nesting in that box. New or young employees are plotted there because it will take some time for them to understand what's going on. Time and training will cure their inexperience. This chapter focuses on the nesters.

These are the six sure signs of a nester:

1. He doesn't show passion for his work.
2. She doesn't show much interest in improving.
3. He needs support from others to accomplish his basic duties.
4. She protects her job through information hoarding.
5. He measures hours, not productivity.
6. She is willing to work hard, provided her incentives increase.

Here's how to help move potential stars to the star box:

- Train and/or coach them.
- Clarify your expectations.
- Change their roles.

Navigate the Wrong Fits
(The "C Box")

"First you build the team, then you build the torture chamber for underperformers."

—Jarod Kintz, author of *This Book Is Not for Sale*

No matter how long you've been at this, and how great your hiring systems are, the time will come when you make a mistake and let a person through the net who shouldn't be in your company. The main difference between toned, fit companies and flabby, lazy companies is that the fit ones recognize the problem quickly, fix it, and move on, whereas the flabby ones allow the wrong fits to stay indefinitely, wreak havoc, and hurt all their best people.

Picking the wrong person is a common mistake. We've all made it. Don't let your fear or your pride prevent you from dealing with the situation. Take action, learn from what happened, and then get over it and move on; give up all hope of having a brighter past.

I made my first important hire when I was a young executive in a growing business. I had to find a manager for a failing corporate store that was bleeding cash. The CEO of the company was absolutely manic to solve the problem, and I felt the pressure to find a solution—fast.

We had no hiring procedures, so I posted an ad and began interviewing candidates. On my second interview, I hit an absolute goldmine; the candidate was a gift straight from heaven—and on only my second try, too! Nobility forced me to keep it to myself, but I could see that I was really good—possibly a prodigy—at hiring.

He had (he said) run a group of retail stores out east in a turn-around situation and built them into a highly profitable chain. He'd been a gift to other businesses, too, tapping them gently with his golden wand, and transforming them from losers to gems of productivity and profit.

He was older now and looking for something fun to do. Obviously, he didn't need to work, and hated to stoop to discuss anything so beneath his notice as a salary, but he thought that probably a high one would make sense as a matter of principle. I assumed he would probably give it to the homeless.

He was engaging and funny, and said everything I could possibly have hoped to hear. None of this raised a flag in my naïve, rosy-cheeked head, nor had I read Mark Twain deeply enough to know that this guy came straight out of *Life on the Mississippi*. If you're playing poker and you don't know who the patsy is, that's because it's you.

As he left the room, he coyly mentioned that he had some other interviews to go to and hinted he would probably take whatever was offered to him first. I thought about checking his references, but this was pre-Internet and the process seemed daunting. A moment's reflection told me he would be offered a job at his next interview, so, on impulse, I hired him on the spot—and felt great, knowing that I had found the silver bullet that would fix the store and (secondarily) make me a legend in the process.

After he had been in the store for a few days, I began hearing strange stories from the staff. He wasn't showing up; he was lying to customers. The assistant manager told me frankly that she "hated this guy." How could she hate my 63-year-old bald Boy Wonder? I couldn't sleep at night wondering if perhaps I had made a hiring mistake.

Fortunately, I didn't have to wait long to find out. One night before closing, he left a deposit bag in his office, broke into his own store from an upper window, and attempted to walk across the T-bar ceiling to steal the store's cash. He crashed through the ceiling tile onto the concrete floor 20 feet below, set off the store alarm, and was hauled away by ambulance after police investigated the alarm. Not only was he a criminal, he was a stupid criminal, and I was stupider yet: I had fallen for his outrageous story. I was furious at myself and embarrassed that I'd been played for a sucker by a conman.

The 7 Sure Signs a Wrong Fit Is on Board

Are you wondering if you might have someone who, for your company and culture, is just not going to work out? The following signs will make it plain to you:

1. She violates your company's right attitudes.
2. He doesn't care about his work.
3. She oozes negativity.
4. He receives bad reports from good people.
5. Her trajectory is all wrong.
6. He has no concept of time.
7. Your gut tells you something is wrong.

1. She Violates Your Company's Right Attitudes

This is the most reliable and objective way of knowing you have a wrong fit on your hands. Lots of people can learn a new skill and become more productive, but not many can change fundamental values and beliefs that guide their actions through the day.

As we learned in Chapter 3, one of the criteria for finding right attitudes is that violations of them make you angry. Is the behaviour of your potential wrong fit making you mad? If you find yourself angry with her, and not over garden-variety mistakes that everyone makes from day to day, you should have a closer look. If she continues to violate your company's right attitudes on a consistent basis and can't (or won't) change, there's a good chance that you have a C player that needs attention.

2. He Doesn't Care About His Work

This comes out in a variety of ways: spending inordinate amounts of time on social media, encountering "emergencies" that require time off during busy periods, getting afflicted with that peculiar and exotic ailment that flares up at odd times, repeatedly adding an extra day to a long weekend.

"That's not my job" syndrome is an excellent diagnostic tool for sniffing out a C player as well. Doing things apart from his strict list of duties could take extra effort, which is an unacceptable breach of the principle of work/life balance to the C player; another possible reason for this malady is the risk of exposing his ineptitude to other people. Better not to help than to come out of the "incompetence closet" to your coworkers.

3. She Oozes Negativity

It's a bad sign when people spew vitriol around the workplace, even if it isn't related to your company or to their job. The woman who can't stop slagging her previous boss, or the man who drones on and on about the imagined deficiencies of his wife are hard on everyone around them—not to mention that one day you're going to be the past boss, and you'll be talked about in exactly the same way.

The same goes for negativity about the weather, the government, gasoline taxes, the hypocritical and rigged nature of Academy Award voting procedures, personalities of customers, and a plethora of other things that she has no control over.

Negativity is a choice, and as the flu does, it spreads. You don't want the rest of your staff catching this flu, because it's one that they don't get over once they've got a bad case of it, and it can quickly become an epidemic. Deal with the disease before it becomes a full-brown epidemic.

4. He Receives Bad Reports From Good People

On the face of it, "bad reports" seems like a subjective way to find out how a person is doing. But if you're hearing negative reports about a staff member from people you trust, pay attention to the news. Don't let yourself get too caught up in "process," allowing the situation to play out on its own. Bad news travels fast, and if these bad reports are coming from credible people, insert yourself into the situation and monitor it closely to find out the truth for yourself.

As the boss, you're the last to hear these things, so if it's leaking back to you, you know it's been around the mulberry bush multiple times already and everyone else is fully briefed on the situation.

5. Her Trajectory Is All Wrong

From personal experience, I know you can determine the trajectory of a new hire very quickly. Typically you can tell within the first week or two if she feels like a fit. It doesn't take six months or a year to make that determination. You know you have a winner when things just "feel" right. She may not know much yet and she may not have solved any real problems, but you can tell that once she has some knowledge and experience under her belt, she'll be just fine.

When assessing someone who isn't a new hire, but has been in her role for a while, look again at her career trajectory. Is it moving upward, staying flat, or going downward? If it's going up, she's becoming better at what she does, she's getting more engaged over time, and she's becoming more valuable by contributing at a higher level.

If her trajectory is flat, she's showing satisfactory results, but nothing more. She shows up and gets the work done, but you don't see more in her future. But if she shows a downward trajectory and her performance and attitude is actually skidding downhill over time, you have a problem.

When I assess business leaders, it isn't hard to predict with a high degree of accuracy where they'll be in one, three, or five years' time. I just look at their past trajectory, because usually that trajectory will continue into the future. Barring unforeseen disaster, the story of each person's future is already written because of the habits he has developed that will keep him winning for a long time to come. Those moving upward will continue to get better and be more successful; those remaining flat will be in about the same place as they are today, and those moving downward will be worse off in five years than they are today. Given these three simple diagnostics, it's not super-hard to be a consultant.

6. He Has No Concept of Time

If you've ever chosen the wrong line at the grocery store and watched while the cashier stops checking items through so that he could fully engage in conversation with the customer in front of you about whether or not he's having a nice day—and then doesn't begin productively moving his hands again until he's through talking—you'll be able to relate to the frustration of this C player sign.

"Hands and mouth must move at the same time," I tell my kids as we load the dishwasher. "If this is not possible, mouth must cease moving." (#lifeskills)

C players aren't concerned about prosaic things like time and productivity. They live in their own fairy world where there are no deadlines—only rainbows and unicorns. In order to win on the horizontal (effectiveness) axis of the Star Chart, you must have at least some sense of time and urgency.

7. Your Gut Tells You Something Is Wrong

Why is it that you don't have to perform an internal song and dance to convince yourself of your great hires? Because it's self-evident that they're working out and they don't need a cheerleader to help lift their brand! Conversely, when you find that you're trying to convince yourself and others that someone is going to work out in her role, you may be living in denial.

I'm a big believer in listening to your gut. A gut check isn't some arbitrary, capricious feeling that you get when you wake up on the wrong side of the bed. It's a finely tuned sense that you've developed over years that recalls similar situations that you've heard of, read about, or experienced personally. A gut check is your subconscious mind linking these hundreds or thousands of connections into a feeling that's real, and one that you should listen to. It's a way of helping you understand that you've "seen this movie before" and that you also know how it usually ends.

When your gut tells you something's wrong, that's because it is. Don't ignore it.

Taking Action With Your Wrong Fits

Think of your wrong fit—the one who permanently lives in that box on the Star Chart. Now think back to your high school biology class and what you learned about parasites. The goal of a parasite is to latch on to a host that can supply its needs, and stay latched on—permanently. The parasite never wants to take so much that the host dies; that wouldn't be effective. The parasite needs to keep its supply of nourishment flowing. The host might feel constantly tired, but that's fine as so long as it doesn't die, thus ending the relationship. The parasite doesn't give anything, it's only there to take.

In the same way, people who permanently live in the wrong fit box don't care about you. They care about themselves and will not take action to sever themselves from you, their host. If anything's going to change with your wrong fits, it will be because *you* initiate it.

Confront Them

Some wrong fits may not be parasites but have drifted into that box for other reasons. This is certainly the case if you've seen them perform better, and you know they can do it if they want to. These people need your help and your intervention if they're ever going to get back on track and move into a better box.

Often wrong fits are never called out on their behavior. This dynamic, however, is not fair to the leader, the company, and especially the employee. If a wrong fit doesn't know specifically why she's in that box, she has no opportunity to address her issues and fix them.

I once worked with a client who had an employee that he felt was a wrong fit. When we discussed her, he was visibly upset and angry about her attitude and lack of performance. He listed her issues while I listened. She had been with the company, underperforming, for 10 years.

When he was done, I asked, "Have you ever said to her what you're saying to me in kind, but clear, language?" He responded, "Not in so many words, but believe me, she gets it." "How is she getting it?" I asked. "I glare at her every morning when she comes in" was his knowing response.

My sense was that she wasn't picking up on the covert performance review too well.

Act as Their Reality Advisor

Wrong fits stay in a company for many reasons. Often, wrong fits think they're doing great.

Harvard Business Review cites an interesting study that highlights the underperformer's perception of his own performance: "People who lack the skill to perform well also tend to lack the ability to judge performance...because of this 'dual curse,' they fail to recognize how incompetent they truly are.... Teaching poor performers to solve logic problems causes them to see their own errors and reduce their previous estimates of their performance."[1]

A reality advisor is someone who helps a person see beyond his own perception of a situation, to what's really going on. As leader, you need to get comfortable wearing this hat from time to time. When a person is unaware of what's really going on, a crash is imminent, and a reality advisor can help him—and the company—avoid the wreckage that usually ensues.

The further reality moves from the perception of reality, the bigger the eventual crash is going to be.

Think of this reality gap in the context of marriage. Imagine a husband entering the marriage with a large amount of debt. He doesn't want to turn off his potential wife, so he doesn't mention anything about it. As time goes on, the debt grows, as does the incentive to keep it secret. However, one day, the wife is going to find out. She's going to stumble across a bank balance, or get a letter from a creditor, or receive a notice that they have to sell their house to settle the debt. When she finally finds the truth, there's going to be a crash.

Such gaps between reality and perception destroy marriages, and they also turn into major people problems at work. When you have an employee who thinks he's amazing and people all around him disagree, eventually it will come to a sad end. This situation can go on for a long time, but it will end, and when it does, it's going to be expensive, messy, and unpleasant for everyone involved. When the beginning is bad, the end is going to be worse.

Jack Welch famously said, "Protecting underperformers always backfires." At some point, perception and reality are going to collide. It's up to you to facilitate that collision and deal with it before it becomes a damaging, painful issue.

Strategize About Your Options

Sometimes replacing a wrong fit is about timing. It's like a battle strategy. You know the battle is coming, but if you're smart, you choose the time and place of the battle, and you don't allow it to be forced on you by someone else, or by your own emotions that press you to act immediately.

Instead, map out a multi-pronged exit strategy. You should be thinking of strategic questions such as these:

- Have I received the best legal advice?
- Who is going to have a warning "reality talk" with this person?
- How are you going to tighten accountability so that underperformance is called out, giving this person every chance to change?

- What is the best time for him to be replaced, both for you and for him?
- Who do you know who could be a candidate to take over his job?

Start brainstorming to come up with names of people who could one day replace your wrong fit and become your new star.

Cut Your Losses

If you've engaged in multiple reality talks, have been clear in your warnings and you still don't see any change happening, it's time for you to act. Retaining wrong fits is not fair to you, to the company, to their coworkers, or to them.

You've been chosen as leader and coach to do what's right for the team, and this is your moment to gain the respect of all your best people. Football coach Lou Holtz said it best: "Motivation is simple. You eliminate those who are not motivated."

This is a critical part of your job. Let's look for a moment at the far-reaching consequences of not acting when you're certain you have a wrong fit.

The Cost of a Wrong Fit

Letting a wrong fit go is a sad decision—but not a hard one, because there are serious costs to keeping one. In fact, studies show that the cost is much higher than you think.

A sales representative can cost up to five times his annual base salary, a manager can cost up to 15 times his annual base salary, while an executive can cost up to 30 times his annual base salary.[2] Does this seem high to you? What if the true number was half of these statistics? Or a quarter? The expense is still massive. Think about some of the costs involved, small to large:

- Paying severance and the ensuing emotional costs in finally letting them go.
- Running ads.
- Vetting resumes and interviewing candidates.
- Training and orienting.
- Repelling your current stars or causing them to leave.
- Making mistakes, small and large.
- Missing sales through incompetence.
- Missing company-wide opportunities for growth.
- Turning off your best customers or losing them during transition.
- Draining your emotional resources and keeping you from focusing on opportunity.
- Repeating the cycle.

The longer a wrong fit stays, the higher these costs mount, and all that time, he's still there underperforming— and taking a paycheck, too! Companies that have stars in every key seat can be up to 300 percent more profitable than those that don't.

The Simple Difference Between a Bad Culture and a Great Culture

One of the biggest costs of letting your wrong fits stick around is in the damage this does to your work culture. At the end of the day, a great culture is one in which great people who perform well share right attitudes. A bad culture is one in which poor performers are tolerated and allowed to spread their bad attitudes to others.

When stars and potential stars work side-by-side with wrong fits and productive-but-difficults, the better workers come to a few conclusions. First, they see that there's no justice in the world. People can get paid the same as them, have a bad attitude, and underperform at work without consequence. They see the futility of giving their all, because in the end, what does it really matter? Great performance, poor performance: it's all tolerated. They conclude, perhaps correctly, that management doesn't really care or notice.

Do you think that poor performers rise up to match the performance of better players around them? If your answer is yes, think again. The great majority of the time, it's the reverse. The stars see that there's no justice—that effort and attitude don't matter—and they begin to sink on the Star Chart. Eventually some will sag to match the performance of the poorest players, and the stars who have other options (because everyone wants stars) will go to work for your competitors.

Here's the HR recipe for your wrong fits:

- Have a reality talk with them.
- Take appropriate action.

People Action Steps

- Forget "chain of command" structures. Ask people at every level of the business how they're doing and if they have any suggestions for company improvement.
- Benchmark your company's performance against the best company in your industry, and ask yourself how their people compare to yours.
- Write the name of one person who you need to have a reality discussion with and set the date for it to happen.
- Develop a multipronged exit strategy for your wrong fits.

In Summary

Everyone makes hiring mistakes. Smart companies recognize and act on the problem quickly. The key indicators that you have a wrong fit on board are:

1. She violates your company's right attitudes.
2. He doesn't care about his work.
3. She oozes negativity.
4. He receives bad reports from good people.
5. Her trajectory is all wrong.

6. He has no concept of time.
7. Your gut tells you something is wrong.

In my work with hundreds of companies representing a huge variety of industries, I've found that a wrong fit can cost between two and 20 times the person's annual salary, depending on their position. I've also found that companies with stars in every key seat are up to 300 percent more profitable than those without them.

A great culture is one that doesn't tolerate C players, and a poor culture is one that does. Sometimes you have to put on your reality advisor hat, and be the person that kindly and firmly brings reality and perception of reality together, so that your underperformer sees the situation and has a chance to improve.

Letting wrong fits go is a sad decision, not a hard one.

11

Deal With Your Productive-but-Difficults (The "D" Box)

"CEOs can talk and blab each day about culture, but the employees all know who the jerks are. They could name the jerks for you."

—Jack Welch, CEO of General Electric

The D box is the worst box of all for someone to be living in on the Star Chart. It is comparatively easy to know how to deal with folks in the other three boxes: retaining your stars; developing your potential stars. That's easy. Firing your wrong fits is obvious. They neither share your attitudes nor show any productivity; this is a sad decision, but not a hard one.

But what do you do with people who are great workers—really productive in many cases—but whose attitudes are downright despicable? Maybe, in fact, they work circles around their colleagues. Often productive-but-difficults have unique (in some cases almost irreplaceable) skills. The rarer the skillset, the greater the chance that a productive-but-difficult is being incubated. How can you think of losing such a person?

But I'll bet you've already thought many times about doing just that. They wear out the people around them, and they pointedly reject your right attitudes. Thinking about them exhausts you. Whenever there's an eruption, your productive-but-difficult is often in the middle of it, loudly proclaiming his innocence, or sitting in sullen silence.

You don't really trust him, either. To use an analogy from the world of pets, productive-but-difficults are more like cats than dogs. There's no question that you share a bond with your dog. There's loyalty and affection there. But cats are different. Though you sometimes hope your cat may love you, you strongly suspect that the only reason she stays around is because you feed her. If the food source was interrupted, or if someone else offered better food, you wouldn't hear from your cat again.

Productive-but-difficults are like mercenary soldiers—soldiers who fight only for money, who fight for opposing countries and causes, and who change teams without any feelings of loyalty. They're there for themselves and what they get, not because they believe in what you're doing. You also suspect that they're already fighting against you while you're paying and investing in them, and sometimes defending them from the rest of the team.

The 4 Certain Signs of a Productive-but-Difficult

It isn't hard to spot people who live in this box. Following are some sure signs to watch for. (This isn't an exhaustive list, but you may recognize some of these symptoms in people that cause you grief.)

1. She undermines you and your initiatives.
2. He stirs up drama.
3. She thinks only of herself.
4. He displays asinine behavior.

1. She Undermines You and Your Initiatives

When our kids were little, my wife and I used a term to describe disrespect that's just under the surface (there's no doubt it's there) but not so outrageous that it can easily be called out; we called it *micro-disobedience.*

When my youngest daughter was about 3, she got in trouble with her mom for some minor offense. As punishment, my wife gave her a time out in her crib, leaving our daughter in room for a few minutes of solitude so that she could weigh the gravity of her crimes in private and emerge, chastened and obedient.

About two minutes into the time out, my wife eagerly gestured for me to come listen silently at the door of our daughter's room. Not wanting to get in deeper trouble, but wanting her displeasure to be clearly known, she was repeating loudly, "I hate you, pretty mommy!"

This is the behavior that productive-but-difficults often display. They don't want a showdown, but they *do* want you to know that they don't respect you (or a coworker), and they communicate it in subtle but unmistakeable ways. You have the strong feeling that, even though they're great workers, they're also working to undermine everything you've tried so hard to bake into your culture.

The truth is that some people are only happy when they're rebelling. In some cases, it's due to immaturity; in others it may show an independent streak that, in the right context, could be a tremendous asset. These folks should (and do) consider self-employment.

Lots of celebrity CEOs would make horrid employees. How would you like Steve Jobs to be your production supervisor? He would be erratic, imperious, unyielding, impossible, and utterly hopeless as an employee. But as CEO he might make the company a billion dollars.

2. He Stirs Up Drama

Productive-but-difficults can be toxic personalities who enjoy getting into big, dramatic, ick-splatting social catastrophes—like the bad kid in your class in middle school. These massive upsets meet some of his basic social needs; they prove he matters. Attention is the goal, and it doesn't matter whether it's good or bad attention—just so someone's noticing.

For some people, big drama actually equals intimacy. The fact that you care enough to enter his gross, complicated world on his terms is something he enjoys. He mistakenly believes this is how to get closer to someone else. "People who hurt the most, hurt the most." People in pain sometimes enjoy causing other people pain, because it provides a distraction from their own miserable circumstances.

Or, as George Bernard Shaw said, "I learned long ago never to wrestle with a pig. You get dirty, and besides, the pig likes it." Drama is exhausting; it wearies those who have to watch the play every day, and creates an atmosphere of distrust and insecurity throughout the business.

3. She Thinks Only of Herself

The Copernican revolution was the stunning change of thinking that occurred when humanity first realized that the sun, not the earth, was the center of the solar system. The productive-but-difficult needs her own personal Copernican revolution, because she believes the mistaken notion that everything revolves around her.

Productive-but-difficults lack maturity and aren't able to see situations from another's perspective. If they have a conflict with a coworker, it's because the coworker is a bad person.

They also look first to their own interests, whether that's getting paid more money or having "lord of the manor," dictatorial control over their own area. They do whatever it takes to guard their own interests.

4. He Displays Asinine Behavior

A lot of profane adjectives can be used to describe the low-lifes that indulge in the wide variety of witless and idiotic behaviors available to the productive-but-difficult. These include bullying and harassing; making cutting, sarcastic, or crude and creepy sexual remarks; acting like outrageous turds in order to prove a point; throwing hissy fits and temper tantrums or having "clam-ups" where they don't talk to others for days.

Asinine behavior is catch-all phrase I'm using to describe a bizarre cornucopia of crazy conduct. Like the guy who loves getting "a reaction" from the women in the office by ogling/talking to them while wearing sexually explicit, graphic "joke" T-shirts, or the guy who looks for a chance to freak out on new hires to maintain his "leadership" position, or the lady who "confidentially" throws rival colleagues under the bus, then backs up the bus and runs them over once more for good measure, or the guy who writes and leaves behind weird, unsettling poems for his colleagues to discover. (These are all true stories.) The possibilities in this category are endless. You know it when you see it.

Like wrong fits, productive-but-difficults don't have much self-awareness. Although they may have some idea that people around them are unhappy with their behavior, in their heart they think they're amazing. And far from imagining that they could be fired, they assume they've reached such a pinnacle of peak performance that the company would never survive without them. That's why they feel free to flout your company's right attitudes with impunity. They know—or at least they think they know—that they're indispensable.

Confronting Your Productive-but-Difficults

You need to give your productive-but-difficults every opportunity to change their attitudes. Do this by confronting their behavior—clearly and kindly.

I once worked with a client who had a productive-but-difficult in a role, and though his performance was, in some respects, good or even very good, my client was sick of his brittle and superior attitude, and was on the verge of firing him.

I asked the leader if he had ever explained to this employee, in clear terms, why he was showing up in the productive-but-difficult box, what he had to do to change it, and what would happen if he couldn't (or wouldn't) change. He said, "Yes, I've told him many times." But he also asked me if I would sit with him one last time to see if he could be rescued. Most leaders hate firing people.

So we sat down together, and I asked the employee where he saw himself on the Star Chart. He pointed to the top right corner of the chart. In other words, he was such a gifted star that he couldn't envision any way that he could get any better.

I advised him to take a deep breath, and then showed him where his employer saw him on the Star Chart. Showing the employee's place on the chart communicated the leader's meaning beyond doubt. This is a big part of the value of the chart. He was gobsmacked. Next, I asked him if he wanted to stay with the company, and if he was willing to do what it would take to get in the star box. He strongly wanted to stay and professed a commitment to do whatever it took.

I then asked him if he could think of any behaviors that might be relegating him to such a bad position on the chart. He thought for a bit and then responded tentatively, "Maybe it's because I don't suffer fools gladly?" I then asked him, "Is that code for you being difficult and abrasive with people you don't like?" He paused and, after a bit, smiled and agreed that he needed to own that.

We ended up with a mutual understanding about the issues that were keeping him in the productive-but-difficult box, and made a clear plan for how he would journey to the star box. His first step (his idea) was to take home-baked treats to the various departments that he interacted with, apologize, and ask how he could be of better service.

Deathbed conversions don't often stick, but last I checked on this guy he was still with the company. The owners, who once wanted his head, were now brainstorming about how to retain him.

Reprimand Them and Act as Their Reality Advisor

I discussed how to give reality advice in Chapter 10. The same advice applies to your productive-but-difficult. In short, you need to articulate two things: (1) the reality of the situation and (2) the employee's skewed perception of reality. The further these move apart over time, the bigger the eventual collapse is going to be. Your job as leader is to bring them into line with one another *before* the big crash occurs and your other employees suffer the collateral damage.

But when dealing with productive-but-difficults, there's another piece of advice: They must be told explicitly that their behavior will *not* be tolerated.

Coach Them if They're Willing to Change

Someone with the right attitude, intelligence, and personality fit can learn almost anything with the right coaching and training. But it's pretty hard to teach someone an attitude, unless they're very young and/or very teachable.

I'm a big believer in trying to shock productive-but-difficults out of their poor behavior. There's nothing to be lost, because anyone nesting in the bottom half of the Star Chart doesn't have a long-term future in the organization. Why not give them an opportunity to change?

I once worked with a medical services firm that had a highly specialized physician who was virtually irreplaceable. Truly, just a handful of people in the world have his specialization, yet this guy was very hard on people around him. He always had to be the smartest person in the room and viewed support staff as minions who were there only to do his bidding. He was condescending and rude, and sucked the oxygen out of any room he entered.

One day the medical director met with this physician and described how his actions affected the workplace. He was taken aback. He really was unaware of the situation. At a follow-up meeting, two support staff members described how difficult life was due to some of his behaviors. One of the women cried. After some coaching, the physician showed genuine remorse, apologized, and pledged to change.

I always recommend confronting your productive-but-difficult with his behavior and showing him how it affects others. You might be surprised to find that he cares more than you think.

Cultivate Options for Succession

When warning and coaching haven't worked, the next step is to try to isolate your productive-but-difficult from others as much as possible. Your productive-but-difficult may have figured out along the way that she gets her best results when working alone. Often these personality types prefer to work by themselves anyway, probably because their level of genius is hard for others to understand, so limit her interactions with the team even more. It's not ideal, but this stopgap measure will buy you some time.

As much as possible, begin to document her job. Knowledge is power, and if all of the knowledge resides in that person's mind, you're held hostage to her and her terrible behaviors. You may have no idea what she's actually doing that's working. You must download that knowledge onto paper, so that someone else can take over that role in the event it becomes necessary.

Finally, get working on building a bench of people who could one day replace your productive-but-difficult. "The graveyard is full of indispensable people," the old maxim says. There's someone out there who has the attitudes, knowledge, and skills that you are going to need. Start looking early.

Keep your eyes open when reading industry journals, attending trade shows, or running into outstanding people in other industries. If you've gone through the other steps and they aren't working, one day you'll meet someone who will be a better fit. You just need to keep your eyes open.

Help Them Exit With Dignity if They Can't (or Won't) Change

Sometimes, perhaps most times, the productive-but-difficult never gets it, and either leaves or has to be fired. This happens even after all your efforts to intervene and save them. Remember that it's much easier to learn a skill than to change an attitude next time you make a hire.

When this happens, and it will happen, help that person exit with dignity. Let them go when their team isn't around to watch them react. Be firm, kind, and generous. Don't enter into debate with them or rehash why it hasn't worked out. Act on good legal advice and fulfill your obligations to them, thank them for the contributions they have made, and wish them luck in their future endeavours. If this takes longer than eight minutes, you've gone too long.

The Productive-but-Difficult *Leader*

Communication is the biggest issue every growth company faces, and no one is willing to bring things up in front of a productive-but-difficult leader. These jerks are never trusted, and they stifle communication. When communication breaks down, trust leaks away; and once trust is gone, the game of culture-building is pretty much over.

If a productive-but-difficult does stay in a leadership capacity, he'll create a tight oligarchy of similar people under him who will feel empowered to impose their own despotic reign of terror, and the best people will also leave (of course).

Life's too short to work for a productive-but-difficult leader or his henchmen. Eventually the cost to the organization will outweigh any benefits he brings to you in productivity.

How should you handle "indispensable" productive-but-difficults?

1. Confront them and act as their reality advisor.
2. Coach them if they're willing to change.

3. Isolate them and cultivate options for succession.
4. Help them exit with dignity if they can't (or won't) improve.

People Action Steps

- Estimate the actual cost of your productive-but-difficults. How many customers have they turned off? What have their mistakes cost? What could you produce if you didn't have to deal with them? Put a number on it.
- If a star leaves you, perform an exit interview with them to find out why they left. Make sure it isn't because of a productive-but-difficult.
- Cultivate options for every key seat in the business. Always be on the lookout for great people. The strongest lever in negotiating is the ability to walk away, and you can only do that when you have other options.
- Hire slowly and carefully. In my experience, leaders spend 75 percent of their time working with non-stars, and 2 percent of their time vetting new hires. Taking the time to vet new hires ensures that you'll be spending less of your time working with non-stars.

In Summary

It's very hard to decide to take action to lose a productive-but-difficult, because he's good at what he does and is very productive. However, he's like a mercenary soldier and you don't trust him; plus he's hard on you and the people he works with.

The four certain signs of a productive-but-difficult staff member are:

1. She undermines you and your initiatives.
2. He stirs up drama.
3. She thinks only of herself.
4. He displays asinine behavior.

A productive-but-difficult in a leadership capacity is a disaster. She stifles communication because she's not trusted, and people won't tell the truth while she's in the room. If she remains in leadership, she'll only inspire a few productive-but-difficults under her to act the same way. The good people are likely to leave.

12

Learn Team Leadership Skills From Parenting

"I don't believe in beating my kids. So I make them wear a Justin Bieber shirt and Crocs to school so the other kids will do it for me."

—Adam Sandler, American comic and actor

I have had more than one client refer to their business team as a "family." It's true, too, and in more ways than one. As a parent of four kids, I can tell you that business coworkers and family members behave similarly in many essential ways, such as tattling on each other; fighting over toys; getting into various spats that flare, cool to embers, and then flare again; griping over unfair workloads; leaving jobs half-done; and causing parents untold worry and consternation.

Business teams can also mirror families in positive ways. They are capable of pulling together against a common threat, sharing laughter and camaraderie, learning to show grace for personality differences, and causing parents to feel deeply rewarded as they mature, grow, and learn to work together.

Parents are constantly talking and strategizing about their kids. Business leaders do the same about their staff. Parenting and team leadership are two of the toughest things you will ever try, and for many of the same reasons. Like parenting, leadership isn't for everyone; but if it's the game you've chosen, these eight lessons apply directly from one to the other.

The Eight Leadership Lessons

1. Rules without a (proper) relationship leads to rebellion.
2. There is a big difference between power and authority.
3. Have a few standards, and stick to them.
4. Be consistent.
5. Ultra-strict and ultra-lenient parents don't produce the best results.
6. Praise in writing; rebuke verbally.
7. Start with people where they are, not where you want them to be.
8. Set the right tone, and everything will take care of itself.

1. Rules Without a (Proper) Relationship Leads to Rebellion

This adage is true, provided the word *proper* is inserted. Any wise parent knows that laying down the law to children outside of a context of a trusting relationship doesn't work; it only makes children bitter and rebellious.

These same parents know that their goal is to have strong relationships with their children based on mutual respect and boundaries, not to try to build peer-to-peer relationships. You don't confide in your child about your grown-up problems. You both have age-appropriate friendships. Your child doesn't look to you as her prime source of friendship, nor do you look to her for that.

On that basis, you can enjoy a satisfying parent/child relationship. Once she's grown up, she will have earned the right to have a relationship of equality with you, but that doesn't exist when she's a child. Your child has lots of friends, but only one set of parents.

The same is true with the employee-employer relationship. Your employee has lots of coworkers, but only one boss. You actually get rebellion when you delve too deeply into an employee's personal life and *then* try to introduce rules. Your job is to be first among equals, and to find your close friendships elsewhere. The day may come when your employee (like your growing child) moves through the ranks and becomes your equal in role, and then, of course, the nature of your relationship will change, too. The essential question to ask yourself is "Am I too close to this person to be able to call out their bad behavior?" If the thought of it makes you squirm, you may be getting too close.

2. There Is a Big Difference Between Power and Authority

Many times we have had to use power when parenting our kids. "No, I'm sorry, there's no more screen time today" or "No, sorry, you can't go to that person's house for a sleepover." They want it, we don't want them to have it, and we exercise our parental power to force them to do what we want. Many employers rely on only this leadership tool alone. It's a useful tool, without a doubt, but power only represents half the story of how effective leaders operate.

By the time I was in my early 30s, I had worked for two bosses who loomed large in my mind. One was strong, effective, and very skilled in the use of authority; the other was weak and ineffective, and relied mainly on power to get things done. Both taught me unforgettable lessons about leadership.

Mark was the lead pastor at a fast-growing church. He was the genuine article. He cared passionately about our organization and was extremely serious about the mission. But he didn't take himself very seriously at all. He was quick to laugh at himself and hear dissenting opinions. His strategy was to lay out goals for employees, and then have coaching sessions to help them figure out how they would achieve those objectives.

At times Mark used power, saying "No, because I'm the boss and I say so." But those times were rare. Mostly people wanted to follow Mark because they respected his values, work ethic, sincerity, and obvious care for each employee. As a result, he developed many leaders. And even though I haven't worked for him in more than 20 years, Mark still has authority in my life; I maintain our relationship and continue to seek his advice.

By contrast, Joe once told me about his two greatest motivational tools: fear and accountability. His strategy involved clearly outlining what he expected people to do (a good thing), and then publicly warning them about the consequences of failure. He called people out in meetings and dressed them down in the most caustic way. He fired people very publicly, making his booming voice reverberate through the building so that everyone knew he was serious about his standards.

People scurried like terrified hamsters to do whatever Joe told them to do. They instantly folded to his demands, promptly got on board with his plans, and apologized profusely when they displeased him. This strategy worked— that is, until he left the room. That's when vitriol poured out over poor, deluded Joe. He thought he was the Man, but in reality he was both despised and disrespected.

A culture of power produces artificial harmony. It's "pretend," and everyone knows it but the dictator. Because people are afraid to disagree publicly, they do so secretly. In our case, routine shipments to customers went missing. Theft (shrink) was out of control. Gossip between employees and long-time customers eroded Joe's power. Employees conspired to confound Joe's plans.

Then, one day, Joe wasn't there anymore. The owner fired him. There was no going-away party, and I never heard about him again. That's how raw power tends to work. It can make things happen quickly, but weakens relationships, and doesn't build loyalty or positive culture, or affect permanent change in people. The influence of power dies the day you are no longer in a position to force people to carry out your will.

Here are the essential differences between power and authority:

Power	Authority
Weakens relationships	Strengthens relationships
Flows from position or title	Flows from character
Engenders obedience	Engenders loyalty and respect
Makes employees compliant	Develops employees into self-managed, responsible contributors
Builds a dog-eat-dog work environment	Builds a cooperative, synergistic work environment
Works as long as you are in a position to force people to do what you want them to do	Lasts a lifetime

Power helps build the culture you want when that power is seasoned with authority. A wise leader knows that authority flows from respect.

3. Have a Few Standards, and Stick to Them

In our house, just like in yours, we couldn't possibly have standards for everything. But there are a few things that are non-negotiable. When those really important standards are violated, we as parents take action. If we don't, our family culture will start to erode and eventually spin out of control. Some of our standards are:

- Display respect—for each other, strangers, and our property.
- Show a work ethic. If you're a slacker, things will go ill for you at our place.
- Have faith. A life rooted in respect for God and His character is foundational in our home.

Your standards may be different than ours. They may be explicitly stated or implicit understood. There will always be situations the standards don't directly cover, but when we consistently enforce them, the family knows what's expected and knows what boundaries not to violate.

In a company, these rules are called many things: core values, guiding principles, pillars of success, rules of engagement, or right attitudes, for example. It doesn't matter what you call them, it matters that you communicate them and make them live in your organization.

4. Be Consistent

Healthy families have boundaries that clearly establish what is and what isn't acceptable, and these boundaries need to be consistently enforced. When one member of the family is punished for a right attitudes violation but another gets away with doing the same, it hurts everyone, including the one who violates with impunity.

In a business context, when some people are allowed to violate rules with impunity, they—and others around them—get bolder. Soon the stated right attitudes become meaningless. Consistency is key.

5. Ultra-Strict and Ultra-Lenient Parents Don't Produce the Best Results

I worked as a pastor to teenagers and their parents early in my career, and I had the opportunity to observe how parenting styles affected children over time. Though I saw baffling situations, in which the best kids came from the seemingly worst homes and in which the very best homes produced some interesting pieces of work, two patterns were fairly consistent: authoritarian parents and indulgent parents.

Authoritarian Parents

In this family, the children lived in a feudal castle with a king and queen who called the shots and made life very difficult for their poor subjects. Usually it was the fathers who ruled with an iron fist.

The main desired outcome of the authoritarian family was obedience and respect. Kids' lives were laid out for them. These homes were characterized by raised voices and displays of anger. This combination of micro-management and harsh treatment tended to embitter the children, and they often grew into rebellious teenagers who engaged in lots of unhealthy behaviors.

In some cases, the kids would come to their senses somewhere in their 20s, and the families would reunite. In others, the rebellious teenagers grew into rebellious adults and never really recovered. Ironically, while these parents achieved obedience for a time, they never really earned the respect they sought.

Indulgent Parents

In this family, any kind of behavior was okay, just as long as the parents felt liked by their kids and were viewed as "cool." Teenagers in these families might be granted parental approval to engage in dangerous and/or illegal activities, like experimenting with sex, drugs, and alcohol.

Teenagers could decide for themselves what they wanted to watch, read, eat, and wear. They could associate with whomever they wanted, at any time. They could attend any party they chose, and they could address their parents in an insolent way if they felt like it.

These children often spun out of control as they came into their teen years, because even teens want boundaries. These kids tended to engage in all manner of unhealthy behaviors, and sometimes emerged with significant, life-long consequences as a result, including addictions, failed relationships, and surprise children of their own. (By the way, these parents weren't viewed by their offspring as cool, nor were they liked much. More likely, the kids were disgusted by their parents' weaknesses, and were only too glad to walk on them like doormats.)

Your business is no different. Strict, authoritarian leadership produces rebellion and unhealthy behaviors without winning respect. Lenient, indulgent leadership just produces chaos.

6. Praise in Writing; Rebuke Verbally

If you have something negative to say to your child, never write it down. When he has it in writing, he can keep it for the rest of his life and go over it again and again. He can revisit his grievances and hurts, and remind himself why the remarks were unwarranted or unfair.

When you praise, do it in writing. Written praise is very powerful, because your child and can go back to it again and again and be reminded of good qualities and the support and love that he has around him.

The same is true in business.

7. Start With People Where They Are, Not Where You Want Them to Be

My wonderful Norwegian dad was great at so many things, but one thing he wasn't great at was being a mentor or trainer. He didn't have the patience for it, and grossly over-estimated the inborn skill set that his children brought to basic mechanical jobs. His on-the-job carpentry training looked something like this:

Dad: "Trevor, get me that!"

Trevor: "What, this?"

Dad: (with scorn) "No, not *THAT*, the other thing!"

Trevor: (tentatively holding up a tool) "You mean *this* thing?"

Dad: (furiously jabbing at the air while pointing) "NOO! THE! THING! OVER! THERE!"

Trevor: (cringing while holding up another tool) "You mean this thing?"

Dad: (now actually staggered by my stupidity) "Here, get out of the way.... I'll find it myself!"

When someone is new to a complex job, expect them to take a full year to really catch on. If they're at 60 percent within six months, they're probably doing okay. Take a breath and remember all the hours you had to devote to get where *you're* at today. Exercise some patience, and become a mentor to someone where they are.

8. Set the Right Tone, and Everything Else Will Take Care of Itself

When you have a young child, you need to establish the right tone. This may require some discipline in the beginning, but once you've built the proper boundaried relationship, established your rules, and shown consistency in enforcing them and making them "live" in your family, the rest is easy. You don't have to punish your child very often, because she feels secure in her home. She knows what the rules are and how she should behave.

This works precisely the same way in your company.

I have a client who leads a manufacturing business. He and his team have set a tone in which staff live and die by the company values. One of those values is to do whatever it takes to get the job done. The tone at the company is very positive, and overall staff share a can-do attitude. The results are stellar.

One day my friend was short-staffed and a related company sent over two workers to help. They were used to a very different culture that permitted a lethargic work ethic and mediocre results. The first guy didn't last until morning coffee break; the second quit after a couple of days, because it was too hard.

When these fill-in workers went back to their own company, they told their coworkers about their terrible experience and that they would never go back. When the news got back to my client, he exclaimed, "I'm so happy— because we've built a company that only stars want to work for!"

A healthy tone attracts stars and repels non-stars.

People Action Steps

- Evaluate your team relationships. Have you become so friendly with any staff members that you've lost the power to call out bad behavior? If so, re-adjust.
- Ask yourself if any of your former employees still seek out your advice. If not, work harder at gaining respect through authority, not power alone.
- Write short, sincere notes of praise to those who deserve it. You will put gas in their tank for months to come.
- List all the skills you've had to master to get to where you are today. Remember that it took time, and start to teach someone those skills, one by one.

In Summary

1. **Rules without a (proper) relationship leads to rebellion**. Your employees have lots of pals but only one boss; don't fail them by confusing them over which one you are.
2. **There is a big difference between power and authority.** Power forces compliance and weakens relationships, whereas authority engenders loyalty and strengthens relationships.

3. **Set a few standards and stick to them**. Define your right attitudes and enforce them with everyone.

4. **Be consistent**. Don't play favorites and allow some people to violate your rules.

5. **Ultra-strict and ultra-lenient parents don't produce the best results**. The ultra-strict employers produce rebellion, and the ultra-lenient employers produce chaos. Stay in the middle for best results.

6. **Praise in writing; rebuke verbally.** If you rebuke in writing, an employee can review it and nurse the hurt for years to come. If you praise in writing, she can review it for years and grow in confidence and self-awareness.

7. **Start with people where they are, not where you want them to be.** Don't expect your new hires to understand the business like you do. Remember everything you've had to learn to get to where you are today. Instead, meet them where they are, and begin the mentoring process.

8. **Set the right tone, and everything else will take care of itself**. Once your employees understand your expectations, very little discipline will be required.

13

Help Everyone Be Their Best

"Coaching doesn't start with Xs and Os. It starts with believing that players win games and coaches win players."

—Bill Courtney, football coach, movie director, and entrepreneur

We can learn a lot about the importance of coaching from this cautionary tale.

Kevin was a young, aggressive hockey player. He'd played for years and was pretty good, but he was still nervous when he approached his first big tryout. He gave it his all—and was thrilled when he was picked for the team. He showed up on his first day, enthusiastic but nervous, knowing a lot would be expected, but eager to be part of a winning team.

His first day was a surprise. He showed up for practice and found that some of the players were really good, whereas others were not only unskilled, but downright cranky and difficult. They were constantly complaining about how other teams had better uniforms and easier practices. The issue was never addressed, though. Everyone got the same amount of ice time, and nothing was said by the coach in the locker room between periods.

Kevin's first game also brought plenty of surprises. To Kevin's mortification, the other defenseman on his line scored a goal on their own team. But the real shocker was that the coach didn't even notice. Nor did he notice when Kevin scored a hat trick—three goals in a single game—all while playing defense. This was his personal best. A couple of close friends on the team congratulated Kevin, but it turned out that the coach wasn't in the arena at the time, and apparently nothing got back to him, so nothing was ever mentioned.

By the end of the season, Kevin was totally confused by the team. Furthermore, three of his best teammates had left—recruited by a different (better, the gossip said) league and replaced by other, average players. Over the summer, Kevin started to question whether hockey was the right sport for him. Or maybe even sports, in general.

Such is the power of an ineffective coach.

Now let's look at some examples of stellar coaches. You've heard of Muhammed Ali, but probably not his coach, Joe Martin. Nonetheless, Ali would not have been a champion without Martin. The same goes for the Green Bay Packers without Vince Lombardi, the Chicago Bulls without Phil Jackson, or Michael Phelps without Bob Bowman.

Coaching is an indispensable tool. It speeds the progress and heightens the trajectory of a star. With the right coach, significant growth may not take five years; rather, it may take five months, or even five weeks. In short, coaching works. In fact, no team or athlete becomes exceptional without exceptional coaching.

Why Traditional Performance Evaluations Don't Work

Many companies still go through the yearly process of formal performance evaluations. I can tell you with authority that this process is hated by managers and employees alike. Both spend a lot of time dreading it and procrastinating around getting it done.

For the manager, it's a major time drain and a process with potentially unpleasant conflict coloring the edges, but the imaginary business professor in her head tells her that this is something that good leaders do. Managers do performance evaluation mostly out of guilt. For the employee, it's a once-per-year, all-or-nothing report card, often with financial gain on the line. Their palms sweat as they think about it, and their mouths turn to cotton. The ugly side of performance evaluation is that it was, in part, designed as a way to fire people with cause without having to pay severance.

Today, the old performance review structure is tottering. It just isn't very effective. Focusing on coaching for better performance gets results, creating an environment where people step up into the star box.

The 2 Key Criteria of a Successful Coach

If you've ever played sports, you already know that coaching works. And any successful coach demonstrates two key criteria: He expresses care and has standards.

Care

Think about a person who was influential in your life before you were 20. Did he care about you? The answer, of course, is yes, every time. If your motivation to coach someone is to hammer her, don't bother starting. It won't work. If you dislike her, it probably won't work, either.

It's too easy to single out the person you have a problem with and begin to focus on her negative attributes. She will feel it, her confidence will erode, and her performance will get worse. As her performance sags, it will prove to you that you were right to begin with. She will feel your laser beam focus, her confidence will erode further still, and her performance will hit bottom.

If you don't think self-confidence affects work performance, consider the case of Tiger Woods. Woods was unbeatable in golf, the number-one ranked player in the world, until his many extramarital affairs were revealed. This was followed by a humiliating public apology and an eventual divorce from his wife. Over the next several years,

Woods's play was highly inconsistent, dropping to a #992 world ranking at the time of this writing.

It's worth asking yourself if you are contributing to this sort of downward spiral by expecting the worst. Are you addressing poor performance because you care, or because you're fed up? When a person feels that you're down on her, her performance is going to suffer, and your prediction of her failure becomes a self-fulfilling prophecy because you subconsciously did all you could to make it happen. Before you have any reality conversations, change your own attitude. You are there to be a career advocate and a coach. Coaches care.

Standards

As leader and coach, you must insist on non-negotiable performance standards.

This formula (sincere care enhanced by high standards) was likely used by every person who has made a significant difference in your life. Think about it—a teacher, coach, boss, or parent. First, they demanded more of you than you thought you were capable of. Then they made it clear that they were demanding this because they wanted you to be your best. It was for your good, because they cared! That combination is incredibly fertile ground in which young leaders are able to grow.

When I was a young teenager, I got a job working on a local farm. I was a city kid and knew nothing about anything important. I was a bit lazy, utterly unskilled, and, although I had held other minor jobs, this was my first time working with an owner who cared about how things were done, was ferociously committed to keeping his word, and stressed the supreme importance of doing a good job.

One day, Jim announced that he had some errands to run, and told me to complete my list of jobs—but whatever I did, to make sure that I unloaded the hay bales from the wagon into the loft of the barn before going home. So I did a few happy jobs around the shop, where it was nice and cool and the radio was playing. And once I finished those I reluctantly began stacking the hay.

Stacking hay in a loft in midsummer isn't a happy job. It's really hot in there, and super dusty. The dust sticks to your sweat; the dusty sweat rolls into your eyes, making them sting. The bales are heavy, and the hay gets under the neck of your shirt and itches, and sometimes the bales poke through your pants, stabbing you in the leg. It's a hot, sweaty, dusty, dirty, itchy, pokey job—not at all what a young, entitled urban sophisticate is looking for.

So when quitting time rolled around, I was all too happy to take off my gloves and call it a day, leaving the job half done, with one end of the conveyor leaning up against the barn and the other end on the half-full hay wagon.

I went home, had my dinner, and thought nothing more about it. I was puttering around in my room when the phone rang. My dad answered it, and when he called to me, saying that Jim was on the line and wanted to talk to me right away, my heart sank. Jim was a man of few words. Our conversation went something like this:

Jim: "What did I tell you to do when I left the farm today?"

Me: "Hmm? I'm not..."

Jim: "I told you to unload the hay wagon. Did you?"

Me: "Well, ah, it's interesting that..."

Jim: "Come out here right now and we're going to finish this job like it should have been done in the first place."

So I got on my dirt bike and rode out to the farm in the dark. Jim was waiting at the wagon. We loaded the rest of the bales on to the conveyor in silence and stacked it in the loft. Then Jim said, "Sit down."

He proceeded to chew me out. He wasn't going to put up with my lackadaisical attitude toward my work. From now on, I was to run, not walk, from job to job. I was to complete everything I was told to do—thoroughly and without complaint.

I felt pretty low, and rightfully ashamed of my behavior. But then he pivoted, and talked about how much he cared about me, and what he saw me doing beyond the farm in my very bright future, provided I engaged in some attitude modification, and fast. Like immediately. Without delay. He finished by asking me if I would work as hard as I could and with my whole heart for the rest of my time on the farm. I responded with an enthusiastic and heartfelt "Yes!"

I ended up working on the farm every summer through my college years. My work ethic was formed there, and I learned that doing my best was not good enough. I was expected to do whatever it took to finish the job. Jim cared enough to have performance standards. He didn't hesitate to hold me to those standards for my good—because he believed that I was capable of doing more than I believed I was. This was more than just a job to me: it was a foundational life experience.

Care without performance standards equals chaos. Performance standards without care equals rebellion. But care along with clear performance standards creates an environment in which employees can flourish and reach goals they themselves never thought possible.

How the Coach and Connect Method Works

You really don't have to coach your employees. The law doesn't demand it. Your business will function (somewhat) without it, so why invest the time? Well, frankly because the Coach and Connect system works. Here's what it will do for you.

Provides Frequent Feedback

We live in a world where anyone born after 1980 is used to instant feedback about everything. I dropped Facebook after about two months, once I realized that it was actually a part-time job where I was expected to immediately respond to pictures and requests and a deluge of other cyber-detritus. However, I was born before 1980.

I read recently about an app called Snapsure that allows you to take a picture of a piece of clothing that you've tried on in a store, send it to friends from the dressing room, and receive their instant opinions about whether you should buy or not buy.

Younger people are used to constant feedback, whether they are posting pictures, adding their comments to YouTube videos, or critiquing online news stories (but doesn't *my* opinion about geopolitics matter, too?).

Hiring an employee and letting him work for a year before he gets some feedback in his formal performance review isn't terribly effective anymore.

Generates Opportunities for Reality Advice

We all have blind spots. To see them, we need a reality advisor who can step in and kindly inform us about what's really going on. It's an invaluable service. People issues emerge when reality, and perception of reality, begin to drift apart. This problem is most common with non-stars, those on the bottom half of the Star Chart. Often, your best people will rate themselves lower than you would, and your weakest players will rate themselves higher. It's ironic that the people who you would lose first if you had the chance, think that you and the organization would die without them.

A reality advisor can help with a kind and honest discussion about areas in which an employee is doing well and where he needs to grow. Growth only comes during times of discomfort; growth stretches us. When a teenager grows, she suffers growing pains. In fact, when we stretch ourselves in any way—speaking in public, working out, saying sorry, moving to a new job or a new town—it isn't comfortable. Reality stings, but growing self-awareness enables us to become better people.

Offers Encouragement

If you're a leader with high standards, there's a good chance you don't often tell your staff when you're happy with them. This is yet another benefit of the Coach and Connect system. Your stars will leave each of your Coach and Connect sessions beaming.

A real star will do whatever it takes to stay in the star box of the Star Chart and will take a lot of healthy pride in being recognized as a star by you. She will take seriously any suggestions you have for improvement. A real star loves being recognized as a high achiever.

Builds Relationships

You may work closely with a person and yet never discuss things that are most important to you both. Although you may work together all day, you may only be interacting on a very superficial level.

A one-dimensional relationship involves the exchange of texts or email. It's only useful for passing data and information. A two-dimensional relationship involves hearing a voice on the phone or seeing a face by video. A three-dimensional relationship involves sitting together in a room and talking face-to-face.

But even face-to-face working relationships can lack depth. Employees are most engaged when they feel personally known and understood by their direct supervisor. This means taking time to understand their career goals, obstacles they may be encountering, and things about their job that they most enjoy and most dislike. These issues are all addressed during Coach and Connect sessions.

Fosters Career Advice and Mentorship

A Coach and Connect session is your chance to give back, helping others by sharing advice and stories. There are two simple ways to approach this.

First, make a list of the skills and lessons you had to learn to get to where you are today. Share the list with the person you're coaching and start to discuss each item in turn.

Second, when you sit down to talk, ask about the problems the person is encountering. Then talk about them, and share the wisdom you've learned on your career journey.

Sometimes Leaders Need a Coach, Too

You as leader aren't immune from this, either. You've got blind spots just like everyone else, and you need a reality advisor, too. It's okay that you don't know everything. Everyone starts out as an amateur, and no one is an expert at leading people. It's both an art and a skill that you can learn and improve upon. It's better when you acknowledge this fact and seek help from your own coach, paid or unpaid. The Coach and Connect process gives your direct reports an opportunity to give you suggestions about how you can grow, too.

Seeking Reality Advice

I recently went to Mexico with two friends I do business with, and we spent the better part of a day talking about our blind spots—the weaknesses that are obvious to others that we don't see in ourselves. Theirs were easy, and as we talked about each of them in turn, I spoke pretty openly, but kindly, about what I saw as each of their blind spots. They did the same with each other.

Then my turn came. Understand that I'm older than both of them. I teach regular workshops on personality and self-awareness. I'm a coach, and basically I've got it covered. Not that I'm perfect, but I've long ago scoured my psyche clean of any blind spots that may have once been there—or so I thought.

They started in on their lists, and I felt like Muhammad Ali playing rope-a-dope with George Foreman, taking one unanswered hit after another and doing my best to cover my vital organs. Turns out that I still have plenty of blind spots to work on. I humbly wrote them down and pledged to get back to work on controlling the negative parts of my personality that hurt my credibility with others.

When I got home I told my wife that every person on earth should get to go through the same experience. Although it made me wince, it was incredibly valuable, and, of course, they were right about everything they said. Do you have friends who will go through this exercise with you? If so, seek their advice!

Being Savvy to Ulterior Motives

Most employees don't understand how hard it is to be the boss. It isn't easy to walk into a room, knowing that all kinds of things are being discussed that they aren't privy to. The boss is usually the last to discover things that are common knowledge to everyone else.

Bosses can never be completely sure who their "friends" are, because everyone stands to get something from them. The boss holds the key to their income, their possible perks, their opportunities for promotion, and their pecking order in the organization. Who can be trusted?

When you're the boss, there are three personality profiles you need to be on the lookout for:

1. Spin doctors.
2. Political operators.
3. Flatterers.

Spin Doctors

"Spinning" is re-shaping the perception of an event in a way that advantages the spinner. This happens all the time in politics. When a politician is caught having an affair or spending outrageous amounts of money, his "spin doctors" invent a way to explain this to the world in the best possible light, subtly shifting the blame away from the politician and directing it somewhere—anywhere—else. Spin doctors function the same way at work. All sorts of issues can be "spun" to the boss. These conversations are usually undertaken behind closed doors, where the spinner can exercise maximum control over his message.

Political Operators

Some people excel in the black arts of political dirty tricks, and some of these operators will find their way onto your team. You know that your workplace is becoming political when people state their opinions so they can gain allies, hurt enemies, and advance their own careers. Political work cultures are terribly inefficient, because they waste money and time playing these games. This stuff doesn't help customers or add any value to anyone. It just makes the culture abhorrent. By contrast, in healthy work cultures, people just say what they believe to be true and in the best interests of the company.

Flatterers

Flattery is taking advantage of the fact that bosses are human beings who need encouragement, too. The typical M.O. of a flatterer is to hide his poor performance by ingratiating himself to the boss. We've all seen this guy. He's a suck-up and a "yes man" looking for ways to curry the boss's favor. Every worker in the company knows who this guy is, and they all hold him in contempt. Some bosses, however, are heavily influenced by the flatterers, and can lose the respect of their team by listening to him.

Like most people, the boss wants to be liked and have his efforts appreciated by the team. This makes him especially prone to spin and flattery. Couple this natural human tendency with the reality of having to make calls that are right for the business and unpopular with some team members, and you have a potent environment for politics to take root.

• • •

As leader, you can do a number of things to protect yourself from spin doctors, political operators, and flatterers. First, find a coach or mentor who you can trust outside of the business to be your confidante. This can be a paid coach, or just someone that you know and respect who is willing to have an occasional coffee with you and provide objective insight and counsel. Second, conduct group meetings whenever possible. Spin doctors and flatterers in particular hate meeting in groups, because they know that, while the boss might be deceived, their coworkers and subordinates won't be fooled for a second. For this reason, they're much less likely to try employing their spin in a group context.

People Action Steps

- Ask two trusted friends to tell you your greatest strengths, and your blind spots, too.
- Ask yourself if you bear some blame in the incubation of your underperformers by eroding their confidence and putting them into a downward spiral.
- Stop using email as coaching tool. Real communication happens face-to-face; email is only useful as a tool to pass along information and data.
- Hold group meetings to neutralize the dark arts of the spin doctors, political operators, and flatterers.

In Summary

Traditional employee evaluations don't work because they're too infrequent, and are used as a report card, not a coaching tool. Coaching works when it incorporates two elements:

1. **Care.** Coaching will only be effective if you sincerely care and want to help. If you're down on the person you're coaching, you're wasting your time.

2. **Standards.** You must uphold non-negotiable and clear standards and expectations with employees.

If you care but have no standards, you'll be viewed as weak and ineffective. If you have standards and don't care about your people, you'll be viewed as mercenary, and your voice will have little effect. But when you combine care with standards, you create a powerful environment where your growing leaders will thrive.

Why use the Coach and Connect method? The law doesn't demand it. Your business can run without it. You do it because it:

1. **Provides frequent feedback.** Employees (especially younger ones) live in a world where most feedback is instantaneous. They expect it and will wilt and underperform without it.

2. **Generates opportunities for reality advice.** We all have blind spots—weaknesses that we don't see in ourselves—and reality advice helps your employees to grow in self-awareness.

3. **Offers encouragement.** Strong leaders often forget to praise and encourage those who report to them. Coach and connect provides an opportunity to encourage your team.

4. **Builds relationships.** Even though you may work together all day, you might not discuss the most important things that motivate your

team members. Coach and Connect sets the stage for those discussions to happen.

5. **Fosters career advice and mentorship.** Coach and Connect is the time when you can pass on what you've learned to someone else, helping them grow to be better employees and human beings.

You need a coach, too! A coach gives you the reality advice you need, points out blind spots, and provides a safe place to talk about your business issues. A coach helps keep you immune from:

- **Spin doctors:** Employees who find a way to point blame away from themselves.
- **Political operators:** Employees who state their opinions to gain allies, punish enemies, and advance their own careers.
- **Flatterers:** Employees who take advantage of your need for support by flattering you, thereby eroding your credibility with your team.

14

Master the Coach and Connect Concept

"A coach is someone who tells you what you don't want to hear, who has you see what you don't want to see so you can be who you have always known you could be."

—Tom Landry, ranked as one of the most innovative coaches in NFL history

Win before you begin.

Before you Coach and Connect, you need to understand some fundamental and unchangeable rules about people that will guide your interactions with them. Obey them and you'll win; forget them and you won't.

- People trust and believe others who like them and are "for" them.
- People distrust and disbelieve others who they perceive to be against them.
- People will never change until they feel understood.

- Everyone approaches situations thinking "What's in it for me?"

Before you Coach and Connect an employee, ask yourself how you feel about this person. Do you like her? Are you really trying to help her, or are you trying to put her in her place? If you aren't sincerely trying to help, you're wasting your time, because your coaching attempts won't work. She won't be able to hear what you're trying to say if you aren't for her.

When perception and reality meet, reality loses.

Maybe you're for her, but she perceives you to be against her. This is something that you need to clarify in words. I always let the person I'm coaching know that I am her career advocate. I don't imply that; I state it in words. I want her to win, and that's the reason I'm talking to her. Unless she believes that, and unless your sincere motive is to help her, you won't achieve much.

A Coach and Connect session, as a rule, should take about 25 minutes. If it's your first time using the Coach and Connect form it may take longer, but once you've gotten used to it, it's not a big, formal deal, just a quick time to, well, Coach and Connect! Here's what the form looks like:

COACH AND CONNECT

NAME: _____ DATE: _____

1. What went well, and what could have gone better for you this quarter?

2. Optional conversation starters.

   What steps are you taking to:

   - Be happy?
   - Find meaning in your work?
   - Be fully engaged?
   - Build positive relationships?
   - Set clear goals?
   - What's one thing you would change around here?
   - What are your career goals?

3. STAR CHART PLOTTING

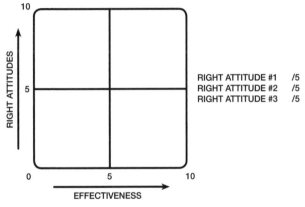

RIGHT ATTITUDE #1   /5
RIGHT ATTITUDE #2   /5
RIGHT ATTITUDE #3   /5

4. The Commits:

   - How can I help?
   - Any suggestions for me or the company?
   - Anything I should know about?

Conducting a Successful Coaching Session

Compared with other performance review tools you've used, Coach and Connect may look pretty bare-bones. But the goal of the Coach and Connect session is to develop a positive relationship, make a commitment to each other around next steps, and have a reality conversation. When the Coach and Connect session is finished, the employee will be really clear about where she stands in the company.

Anyone who's worn glasses with an old prescription knows the huge difference between "kind of clear" and "really clear." Coach and Connect will help you to be *really* clear.

Let's walk through the steps to take to conduct a successful coaching session.

Step 1: Decide on the Outcome You Want

Coach and Connect is a time to engage in conversations that don't normally arise, even though you may work closely together. The person you're coaching should leave his Coach and Connect session with:

- Clarity on where he stands.
- Knowledge of exactly what he needs to do next in order to be even better.
- A positive feeling that he can achieve what's being asked of him.

If there's a tough conversation to be had, think through what you want to say before you get in the room together.

Step 2: Create an Environment of Safety

A safe location is a physical place that represents neutral ground. That means the coach is not in the "power position"—no sitting behind desks or meeting in a space in which the leader has the power. It also means a place where there is some privacy, and you can both talk without fear of being overheard. Typically that means a neutral meeting room, a coffee shop, or even an outdoor picnic table. Be creative.

Assure the person that you won't be discussing your conversation with his coworkers and that he can feel free to speak his mind. Make the person being coached feel safe.

Step 3: Let Him Talk

Before a person can hear anything from you, he has to "empty out." If you begin by talking, he won't hear much of what you have to say. It's quite simple if you follow the form. Ask him, "What went well, and what could have gone better?"

The Coach and Connect form has an optional section for conversation starters. If your employee isn't very talkative, or if you're stuck for something to ask, choose a question or two from this section to "prime the pump." Until he starts talking, the Coach and Connect hasn't really begun.

There is a big difference between active and passive questions. An active question is one where the responder has to take some responsibility for his actions. Imagine the responses that you would receive to the question "Do people treat you well around here?" You would likely get a set of grievances. However, if you ask an active question such as "What are you doing to build positive relationships around here?" the onus is placed on the responder, not you.

Many people are under the misguided notion that someone else can make their life work for them. One day their spouse will wise up, meet *their* needs, and make *them* happy. One day, the world will figure things out and give them a set of circumstances (maybe winning the lottery) that will finally make things better. And one day, *one day*, maybe someone at their workplace will figure them out and serve up just the right conditions on a silver platter so that they can be happy.

Of course, this is a myth. The truth is that it's up to you to make yourself happy. No one can do that for you. Two unhappy people who want their needs met don't come together and make a happy marriage. Lottery winners are generally worse off *after* they win. And no workplace is going to make someone happy. Deciding to be happy is a choice that everyone has to make for themselves. As my mom said to me growing up, "If you want a friend, be a friend." In other words, take action if you want things to change.

Use active questions to help your team member understand that he has to take action if he wants to have a positive work environment. He has to try his best to be happy, build positive relationships, find meaning, and set his own goals. You as the coach can help him, of course. You can advise him and be a sounding board and try to remove obstacles that are getting in his way, but it's not your job to make someone else happy. Free yourself from that load of guilt.

Step 4: Ask Him to Plot Himself on the Star Chart

Begin with the vertical axis. Ask him to score himself out of five on each of your company's right attitudes. Based on his scores, ask him to estimate where he would fit on the vertical axis of the chart.

Next, ask him to estimate his level of effectiveness, and plot the number on the horizontal axis of the Star Chart. Finally, encourage him to put a mark on the chart where the two axes come together. Ask him to elaborate on why he placed himself where he did.

During this time, you need to hold your tongue. You may completely disagree with what he's saying, or believe that his remarks are unfair, unkind, blinkered, or unwarranted. Resist the impulse to correct him, defend yourself, or change his perception of reality. Just let him talk, and concentrate on being an active listener.

Active listening means:

- **Paying attention.** Shut off your phone, look directly at the person speaking, and listen attentively to make sure you understand what he is saying. Don't gaze out the window or glance at your watch or roll your eyes or fiddle with your pen or disappear into your favorite fantasy. Don't start mentally preparing your rebuttal. Really listen.

- **Using body language to show you're interested.** Sit forward a little bit when he speaks. Nod when appropriate. Smile, and keep your posture open and inviting. Don't cross your arms, clench your fists, scowl, glower, drum your fingers on the desk, or make harrumphing noises. Being civil is not good enough. Likewise, avoid leaning back on your chair, engaging in gaping yawns, sucking at your teeth, cracking your knuckles, doodling with a pen, blowing your nose, and so on. Encourage the speaker to continue, using small comments like "okay," "yes," and "uh huh." Make notes if you wish.

- **Asking clarifying questions.** Use open phrases such as "Is this what I hear you saying...?" "When you say this, do you mean...?" "Help me understand that better," and "Could you elaborate on that point?"

- **Deferring judgment.** As tempting as it may be to interrupt, this is not your moment to pontificate or argue with the speaker. Resist these temptations; only listen, ask clarifying questions, and take notes.

Step 5: Plot Him on the Star Chart

Now it's your turn to plot him on the Star Chart. It's critically important at this stage that you be honest, specific, and kind.

Let's start with the first criteria: be honest.

When you're dealing with a star, or even a potential star, this isn't terribly hard. Just tell him the truth. Elaborate on areas in which you see him as strong, and areas in which you think he could grow. Explain why you place him where you do on the chart. Mirror the process that he just completed, beginning with right attitudes and then moving on to effectiveness.

Only the truth sounds like the truth. If you're making things up to soften the blow, or trying to hide the truth, it won't sound real, and the employee will see through your efforts at concealment.

Unaddressed people issues brew like volcanoes. Before the eruption, everything on the surface looks normal. The mountain is placid and calm, and it's all business as usual. However, underneath this placid exterior is so much foment, heat, and upset that rocks are being liquefied; you just can't see any of this from the outside. Then, seemingly without warning, the magma from beneath the surface bubbles up and there's an explosion. This can happen externally in a verbal flare-up, through stress leave, a sudden acrimonious departure, or some other radical response.

Explosions can also happen internally. Internal explosions can include affairs, substance abuse, and depression.

Whatever form it takes, when the explosion is over, a lot of dead, barren ground is left behind. The barren ground can be a person who carries hurts for a lifetime, a boss who feels cynical and burned forever after, or a team left wondering why a coworker was fired without warning. All of this could have been avoided if the lava had been slowly drained, rather than allowed to build up to critical, uncontainable levels.

So be honest. This honesty should not come from a mean or hurtful place, but because you care and want the situation to improve.

Once you've described his positive qualities, avoid using the word *but*. The *but* will negate in his mind all the positive things that you've just elaborated. Instead, substitute *but* with *and*.

And now the second criteria: be specific.

As much as possible, give examples to support your reasons for placing him where you did. If he scored very high on the attitude portion of the chart, tell him why, and be specific. "That day last month when Customer Jones blew up in the store and you handled his concerns so professionally is a great example of how you live out our right attitudes" is better than "You display a very professional attitude." Your employee will be happy (and maybe astonished) that you noticed.

The same is true with areas for growth. "Last month when you came in late three days in a row, it was hard on the team because they all had to work late as a result" is better than "You could grow in the area of punctuality."

And the final criteria: be kind.

Everyone has a huge, ego-based reluctance to hear negative things about themselves, and yet we all have areas in which we need to grow. These things need to be said.

Think about how *you* react when you're confronted with things about yourself that aren't great. Have you ever been defensive or irrational? You know you have.

The best way to help the receiver hear your comments is to be kind. That doesn't mean excusing bad behavior, or saying that something was okay that really wasn't. But being nice is free, and you should be nice whenever possible. That means not being overly picky and not sweating the small stuff.

Step 6: Ask for His "Commits"

At this stage, you've had a good, honest conversation and your employee has a clear understanding of where he falls on the Star Chart. Even if he disagrees, he's heard your perspective. Now it's time to make some commitments to each other about how things will before the next Coach and Connect session.

What's his "commit"? Will he commit to being punctual, increasing quality in his area, changing his attitude toward a coworker, or repairing a relationship that's broken? He should leave with a commitment that he's willing to keep.

As the coach, you have a responsibility here as well. And this involves asking three straightforward questions:

1. How can I help?
2. Do you have any suggestions for me or the company?
3. Is there anything I should know about?

Question #1: "How Can I Help?"

Communicate your commitment to him. Will you look into further training or coaching for him, or help him to locate tools or equipment that will make his job easier? Will you help him by removing an obstacle that keeps him from doing his job right every time? Will you go with him to help repair a relationship? Or maybe you'll let him know if he starts engaging in some destructive behaviour that you've discussed, but that he doesn't notice in himself.

Whatever it is, ask how you can help so that you can make your "commit," too, and then write them both down on the Coach and Connect form.

Question #2: Do You Have Any Suggestions for Me or the Company?

It's at least theoretically possible that you're not perfect either, and now's the chance for your employee to have his say. You've made your comments, and it's only fair that he has a chance to speak his mind, too. Listen without prejudice and see what you can learn.

Question #3: Is There Anything I Should Know About?

Interesting things come out when this question gets asked, and when employees know it's coming and can think about it ahead of time. It's an opportunity for them to be a whistle blower if necessary, or just to tell you something important that you don't currently know. Some answers that I've heard when this question is asked are:

- One of the male leaders in the company is hitting on, and otherwise creeping out, the women who work alongside him.
- Someone is stealing money from the till.

Or more routine, but important things like:

- I want to go back to school and won't be here in the fall.
- I've been offered a job by another company and don't know what to do about it.

You just never know what will come out when you ask this question, and it's a good one to throw in. Once you've moved through the questions on the form, you're finished the Coach and Connect session.

How to Handle Disagreements About Star Chart Placement

At times a person will disagree with your placement of him on the Star Chart, and even after you've had an open discussion about it, he may still disagree, even passionately.

Imagine how you would handle this if the same thing happened on a baseball team and you were the batting coach. Let's say your team member was striking out too often, and you sat down with the player and told him that he needed to change his stance at home plate so that he could achieve better results. Imagine that the player then told you that you were wrong, he was right, and he was going to stand however he liked, regardless of what you thought.

You would have some options, depending on your level of authority. You could choose at that point to appeal to a higher authority, and involve the head coach to get a second opinion on the matter and mediate a solution. If you were the general manager and held ultimate authority over the team, you could choose to tell your player that he was free to stand at the plate however he chose, just not while on *your* team.

If someone strongly disagrees with your placement, it's actually a good thing, because it's exposing a problem that needs to be addressed. It's like an early medical diagnosis: It's not what you want to hear, but if there's an issue there, you want to know about it as soon as possible. It shows that a Coach and Connect session is timely and necessary. However the situation resolves in the end, Coach and

Connect is the first step to breaking the logjam. Without it, this reality gap is going to increase and get worse, and end badly at some point in the future.

Engage in unfiltered dialogue with the employee. Involve higher levels of authority if necessary. Make sure you sort out the reality gap so that you can have a smooth-functioning team that operates without silos, turf wars, or secrets.

People Action Steps

- Try plotting yourself on the Star Chart before plotting anyone else. Be honest. Be specific. Be kind.
- Coach and Connect with your senior people first. Let everyone know that every single person in the company will go through the process.
- Gather positive stories to share with your A-boxers. The point of the interview is to encourage them and make them happy they chose to work with you.

In Summary

Win before you begin your coaching session. Remember these immutable laws of human interaction:

- People trust and believe others who like them and are "for" them.

- People distrust and disbelieve others who they perceive to be against them.
- People will never change until they feel understood.
- Everyone approaches situations thinking "What's in it for me?"

When doing a Coach and Connect session:

1. Decide on the outcome you want. Win before you begin.
2. Choose a safe location to coach in—a neutral space.
3. Let him talk and "empty out."
4. Ask him to plot himself on the Star Chart. Listen without judgment.
5. Plot him on the Star Chart. Be honest, be specific, and be kind.
6. Ask for his commitment for the future. What will he do to make a better workplace?

Also ask how you can help, if he has any suggestions for you or the company, or if there's anything you should know.

15

Handle Those Tough HR Conversations

"The single most important thing is to shift [your] internal stance from 'I understand' to 'Help me understand.' Everything else follows from that."

—Douglas Stone, author of *Difficult Conversations: How to Discuss What Matters Most*

Dealing with the employees in the top half of the Star Chart is easy. These are people you like. They share your right attitudes and they're good people. The bottom half of the Star Chart is a different story. Whether they're productive or unproductive people, the conversations can be unpleasant.

In fact, there's a tremendous temptation at this point not to tell the truth, but to soft-pedal what you have to say. "It's too icky," you'll tell yourself. "It's too hard to say what I really believe to be true," or "Putting it out there will only make it worse." This afflicts people at every level of the company, and it's something that you have to push through to be effective.

Because of employer reluctance, an employee often misses the message in a typical performance review. Even though the reviewer knows that the employee is in a job-threatening situation, she doesn't want to give too much negative feedback to the employee and risk a scene. So, she scales back, makes a few comments, and assumes that the employee understands that the situation is serious. Meanwhile, the employee has an ego-based reluctance to hear negative things about himself. Because of this, the reviewer's scaled-back comments are further reduced in gravity.

Both leave the same interview with very different viewpoints. The reviewer believes that she has kindly but strongly implied that the employee had better change and that the situation is serious. The employee leaves feeling that, though there are some areas of disagreement between him and the boss, basically he's fine. He chalks it up to a "difference in philosophy" or a "personality clash" or just that his boss was overly picky or had a bad day. Such vague conclusions only cause the reality gap to grow.

Conducting a Successful Reality Conversation

Now let's walk through how to conduct an actual reality conversation. Just follow the formula, step by step, in this order:

Step 1: State your facts.
Step 2: Describe the patterns of behavior.
Step 3: Ask for his perspective.
Step 4: Agree on the next steps (his and yours).

Step 1: State Your Facts

Once you've worked through what went well, what could have gone better and finished plotting on the Star Chart, it's your turn to state the facts as you see them. These should be as objective and specific as possible. They may include concerns such as:

- "You have been late for eight of your last 20 shifts."
- "I have received complaints about your level of customer service from two of our key customers."
- "Your sales numbers are 25 percent lower than they were last year, even though your colleague's sales are up by 10 percent on average."

This is a time to state any objective facts you may have. This part isn't about how you or they feel, but what you know to be true.

Step 2: Describe the Patterns of Behavior

Typically, destructive behaviors will pop up again and again in different circumstances, all displaying a similar pattern that may have the same root cause. These might look like this:

- "You've been late for eight of your last 20 shifts, and I've also noticed that you've been late for all of our weekly staff meetings. In

addition, twice I've seen that you've left early
without completing your shift."

- "We've had complaints about your level of customer service from two of our key customers.
You've also been snappy to your coworkers two
times in my presence this month."
- "Your sales numbers are 35 percent lower than
they were last year, even though your colleagues' sales are up by 10 percent on average.
I've also noticed that you seem unengaged and
'down.' You didn't attend our staff meeting,
and your budget was late, too."

You've stated the facts that you know to be true, and
you've elaborated on a wider pattern of behavior.

Step 3: Ask for His Perspective

His bad behavior is likely rooted in feelings, not thoughts.
Until he feels understood by you, he will not be open to
anything you say. Don't assume that he has bad motives by
making provocative statements such as "I can see that you
don't care about your job anymore" or "It's obvious that
you just don't respect people." Instead, ask for his perspective. Use active listening questions such as:

- "Is this what I hear you saying?"
- "When you say this, do you mean...?"
- "Help me understand why you...."
- "Could you elaborate on that point?"
- "Could you talk more about that?"

Listen, not to figure out what to say back, but to really understand the situation. Summarize what you've heard him say, and ask if you're right or wrong about the patterns that you see. Show real interest in hearing his side of the story, and convey your sincerity to him.

Step 4: Agree on the Next Steps (His and Yours)

What happens from here? Is he going to meet with you every week to discuss progress? Is he going to enroll in a class or read a book? Is he going to apologize to someone? Are you going to let him go if he doesn't make progress within three months? For his sake and yours, be very clear about what the next steps are.

The Importance of Clarity

Early in my career I did some work with a family business that was very nice to its employees—so nice, in fact, that they were unintentionally hurtful. By granting too many perks, offering too little meaningful feedback, and establishing zero accountability, they turned some otherwise good employees into lazy, entitled people.

One of the unfortunate recipients of this unintended harm was a person in a sales role who had been in his current job for three years and with the company for more than 20 in various roles. He had underperformed in most of them and been shuffled throughout the company, bumped from manager to manager—each enduring him until they couldn't take it anymore and then passing him on to some-one else. This phenomenon is known as "failing upward."

During his three years in sales, he had never once met his targets. In fact, he hadn't even paid for his seat. In other words, he had cost the company money every single month for the prior three years. He had mastered many parts of the job (consuming coffee, sitting through meetings, keep-ing his bum in his chair for eight hours every day, chatting with admins)—except for the part about inducing custom-ers to buy products.

The owners felt that, this time, something had to be done. No more playing "hot potato." They gave him four months to figure things out, after which they would let him go if he didn't improve. They hired me to help him work through this process. The first thing we did was to establish the targets that he needed to hit so that he could keep his job.

When I met with the employee, we talked, set goals, and did all the things you do when you're working against an important deadline. However, it became apparent in that first meeting that this deadline was important only to me. He was quite relaxed about the whole process. This seemed ironic to me, as I already had a job, while he was facing the prospect of not having one shortly. Shouldn't *he* have been the worried one?

But he didn't see it that way. He felt confident in the knowledge that this irritating process, like the flu, would pass in time, and it was his job to play along through the tedious task of sitting with me each month. I tried my best to convey the seriousness of the situation and convey his employer's resolve to take action if things didn't improve.

The next month, when I came to review his progress I discovered that he hadn't done anything that he had agreed to do the month before—not one thing. So I again played the tape out to the part about him getting fired if he didn't get better, and again made a to-do list with him that he agreed to get serious about.

The third month was the same song, different verse. Nothing done. This time I warned him, "You will be fired next month if you don't get moving! Read my lips! Make some progress!" He was sheepish and acknowledged that he had been lazy but that now he was serious.

By month four, nothing had been done, and I came back, this time with the owner in tow. We sat him down. The owner recapped the situation and, with great sadness, told him that they were going to have to let him go. The guy immediately burst into tears.

Every boss dreads this moment, and no one really knows what to say. So I said, "Can you tell us what you're thinking?" Without hesitating, he burst out, "I can't believe this is really happening!"

This was the moment I learned that denial is not only a long river in Africa—but that you should never underestimate the human species' amazing ability to live deeply in it.

Whatever you're saying, make it crystal clear.

Five Instances When Coaching Doesn't Work

If you're deciding whether or not to pour extra time and energy into someone beyond going through the Coach and Connect process, make sure no roadblocks get in the way of having a winning engagement. Here's when coaching *doesn't* work:

1. When it is offered as an alternative to punishment.
2. When there isn't a deep commitment to change.
3. When the person being coached has a flat (or declining) performance history.
4. When the main emphasis is on listening to the person's feelings.
5. When the person can't (or won't) focus.

1. When It Is Offered as an Alternative to Punishment

Sure, we've all the heard stories about the cranky productive-but-difficult who pulls an Ebenezer Scrooge, sees the light, and is a changed person after being forced into coaching. Sometimes it snows in July, too, but I wouldn't count on it as a regular event.

If, for whatever reason, the coachee isn't interested in getting coached and growing and making progress, it isn't going to work. None of us has the power to make a grown-up do what he doesn't want to do. He'll just have another story of how he "tried that, and it didn't help either."

2. When There Isn't a Deep Commitment to Change

When a person wants to see "a little progress" in an area, it isn't likely that anything will be different in six months. If, for instance, a person has received feedback that she is hard to work with and she acknowledges it but goes no further than just saying the words "I would like to try to get better," she likely won't.

For real change to occur, the concerns not only have to resonate with her, but she needs to make specific, time-based commitments in order to improve. She needs to share these commitments with her coach and her team so that she has accountability.

The person being coached needs to be committed to progress. If she begrudges the time wasted sitting with you through the Coach and Connect process, this isn't an auspicious sign of dramatic life change to come. Think of coaching like applying fertilizer: When applied to a green, growing plant, it speeds things up a lot and is critical to superior growth. When applied to a dead plant, it's a waste of time, effort, and resources.

3. When the Person Being Coached Has a Flat (or Declining) Performance History

Though you're going to Coach and Connect with everyone on your team, reserve your extra mentorship time for those who really want it, and show either a history of, or an interest in, developing an upward trajectory.

If an employee is on an upward trajectory, in all likelihood that's going to continue. If his trajectory is flat or in decline, that's likely going to continue, too. All of the trajectories will continue, in fact, with or without coaching. The upward person is still going to get there in the end. It's just that they will get to their destination a lot faster with coaching. The flat/in-decline person will continue on his path, too. The only difference is that the frustration of attempting to coach him will take at least two years off your life, if you keep at it. And you'll be renowned as a failed coach for your trouble.

I once spoke with one of the top business coaches in the world, and he told me that his secret to success was very simple: Just work with the top people in the world, and they make incredible amounts of progress because of who they are. They're going to be amazing whoever they work with! And then the coach can bask in some of their reflected glory.

The best indicator of future progress is past progress.

4. When the Main Emphasis Is on Listening to the Person's Feelings

Successful coaching is about adding tools and accountability so the coachee can see if she's had good or bad week or quarter, and adjust accordingly. A friend with an ear and a shoulder to cry on is a great thing to have in life, but that's not the job of the coach.

Have you ever tried crying to your football coach about how your feelings were hurt? You wouldn't get his sympathy, because it's *his* job to help you become the person even you didn't know you could be. It's your *mother's* job to listen to you and wipe your tears and tell you that it's all right. Both roles are important; remember which role you're playing.

5. When the Person Can't (or Won't) Focus

For coaching to work, it has to move to the center of the "concern plate." Sometimes that's about timing. If a person (even an upward trajectory person) can't make the time or doesn't have the desire at present to make coaching a priority, it's probably not going to accomplish much.

To increase performance, add structure. Think of how things progress as you move up in a sport. When you play a game of road hockey in the street, you come with your own stick after your homework's done and go home when your mom calls you in for dinner. The rest is made up on the fly.

When you play beer league hockey, you pay some money for ice time, buy some equipment, show up (everyone hopes), and skate around and get sweaty and have a good time. It's more structured than road hockey, and your results are better, too—but not great.

But when you play NHL hockey, structure prevails. Your eating and exercise and sleep habits are structured. The way you play the game is carefully planned and constantly examined. You get regular, immediate feedback about every aspect of your game and how to improve it; as a result, you play at a much higher level.

People Action Steps

- Practice active listening at home before you use it at work. Take your spouse or a friend out for a coffee, shut off your phone, and walk through the steps.
- Find your own coach. You could agree with a friend to coach each other. It doesn't have to cost money to be effective.
- Find a friend who would like to grow. Write down one or two questions that each of you would like to be asked every day, something like "Did I do 100 push ups today?" or "Was I on time for every meeting today?" Text each other a yes or no every night before bed, indicating whether you or not you did it.

In Summary

In a tough reality conversation:

1. State your facts. Be clear about the behavior that needs to change.
2. Describe the patterns of behavior.
3. Ask for his perspective.
4. Agree on the next steps (his and yours). Be really clear on what needs to change for the relationship to work and what will happen next if it doesn't.

Don't waste your time coaching if:

1. It is offered as an alternative to punishment.
2. There isn't a deep commitment to change.
3. The employee's performance history is flat or in decline.
4. You're just going to talk about feelings (rather than press on toward clear goals).
5. The person can't focus on coaching as a top priority.

CONCLUSION

Career Lessons From Trevor

"The only way to do great work is to love what you do. If you haven't found it yet, keep looking. Don't settle. As with all matters of the heart, you'll know when you find it."

—Steve Jobs, cofounder and CEO of Apple

I've learned over the years that your organization is simply a mirror that reflects all of your personal strengths and weaknesses. All the behaviors that you see in your team (things that you both love and hate) are reflections of you and your leadership style. If you're gregarious but sloppy, probably your team looks that way, too. Sales might be strong, but the inside of the business may feel chaotic. If you're a buttoned down, by-the-book type, your organization may get things done right, but feel cold and inflexible to customers.

There's nothing more important than you walking the talk; embodying the right attitudes that you preach to your staff. Speed of the leader, speed of the team.

The 7 Ways to Thrive as a Leader

Having said that, now it's time to take a good, hard look at yourself. How do you think people in your workplace view you? You know they've discussed it. What does your boss think? Or maybe you are the boss, and it's difficult for you to find honest feedback. Here are my suggestions on how to live, thrive, and survive wherever you work:

1. Score yourself based on the "4 Questions" from Chapter 2.
2. Plot yourself on the Star Chart.
3. Work for challenge, not for money.
4. Focus on being great at your job, not advancing your career.
5. Learn to manage your own emotions.
6. Specialize in creating solutions, not in analyzing problems.
7. Develop perseverance.

1. Score Yourself Based on the "Four Questions" from Chapter 2

Question 1: Would your boss enthusiastically rehire you if she could do it all over again? If you're the owner, would you enthusiastically rehire yourself in your position, or would it be better to have someone else in your seat?

Question 2: Do you take away your boss's stress? Or, if you're the owner, do you *cause* stress to the team members around you?

Question 3: If you were to resign, how would your boss feel? How hard would she try to keep you? How would your team members feel if they heard you were leaving and they were going to get a new boss?

Question 4: What if everyone in the business was just like you? Would it be a better or worse place?

2. Plot Yourself on the Star Chart

Once you've plotted yourself, ask your boss/significant coworkers to do the same. Have an honest conversation about where you're perceived to be and how you can get better. Remember: when perception differs from reality, reality loses.

If you're the boss and you're not a star, that's a problem! It's time you upgraded your skills, or adjusted your role so you get to do the things you love and stop doing the things you loathe.

3. Work for Challenge, Not for Money

Taking a job only because it pays well is usually a mistake. The best reason to take a job is because it will develop skills around your natural area of talent. The same goes for leaving a role. The time to leave is when the challenge is gone, not when you can find someone else to pay you more money.

Ironically, when you work in areas of your natural genius, money will follow your passion; and the more you love what you do, the more you'll be paid for it.

4. Focus on Being Great at Your Job, Not on Advancing Your Career

Consider this quote from Bill Gates, Microsoft founder: "Flipping burgers is not beneath your dignity. Your grandparents had a different word for burger-flipping: opportunity."

If you're asking yourself how to make more money or how to get a promotion, you're asking the wrong question. What you should be asking is "How can I be amazing at what I'm doing right now? How can I focus more on the parts of it that I love?"

Once you are clear on what your unique genius is, work hard to find where that genius can best be used. Then find a role that will shape and develop that natural talent, and turn it into a skill so that it can be put to its best use. You'll get better and better at the things that you're already talented at—and what's more, you'll love doing it. Focus on blooming where you're planted, and opportunities will present themselves naturally to you. People always notice (and want) star players.

5. Learn to Manage Your Own Emotions

One of the top reasons that businesses stop growing is because the leader doesn't want to deal with any more draining people problems. If you become known as a person whose presence consistently lifts the energy in the room rather than lowers it, you'll be noticed. If you're one of those people who needs to "vent" to those around them, plan on staying in your current job for a while, or being demoted or moved laterally, far enough away that your current colleagues don't have to listen anymore.

Your emotions can be your own worst enemy if you let them manage you. Don't allow this to happen. Your emotions are a servant of your will, not a helpless victim of your circumstances.

6. Specialize in Creating Solutions, Not in Analyzing Problems

Problem analysis is a highly overrated skill. Most people can already see what the problem is. They need to know is how to solve it. Even more than that, they need to know *who* is going to solve it.

Make it a practice to come prepared with two or three possible solutions to any problem that you or the team is facing. When you see a miserable, unpleasant problem that no one else wants to touch, speak up and volunteer to fix it. There is always, always, a need for the person who says, "Leave it with me, I'll get it done."

7. Develop Perseverance

Many younger workers grew up getting everything quickly and easily. When they wanted something to eat, the microwave got it ready in a couple of minutes. Praise came easily in a school system that frowned on competition and that didn't allow them to fail any class in which they did poorly. Helicopter parents told them that they were amazing and could be anything they wanted. Social media taught them that friendships were superficial and about "likes," not about relationships. Maybe they also got lots of Christmas presents and a huge haul on Halloween.

These people unconsciously developed the expectation that they would be instantly noticed as a wunderkind and that advancement would come quickly and effortlessly. When it doesn't, they became baffled and disillusioned.

On a recent tour of Israel, our guide (an ex–Israeli military officer) told us that Israeli leaders are made not in the bustle of the cities, but in the desert. We spent a morning walking in the Negev Desert, and there's just nothing there. It's like the surface of Mars (in fact, the movie *The Martian* was filmed in the Negev). Water and food are scarce, and predators are everywhere. But the desert is where the important lessons of life and leadership are learned. It's where leaders learn resilience, self-reliance, fortitude, relational depth, and resourcefulness. Cities teach lessons of superficiality, speed, and artifice. Some of the greatest Israeli leaders (including first Prime Minister David Ben Gurion), maintained homes in the desert to center them so they could be effective when back in the city. Success isn't built on success. It's built on hardship and personal agony, and failure, and sometimes disaster.

I once worked with a CEO who told me that the most important job he had in his life was leading an installation department of a furniture company. For seven long years, he climbed stairs, carried heavy stuff, and worked long hours doing a really tough job with a team of guys who had few, if any, other options in life. It taught him perseverance, work ethic, tenacity, resourcefulness, and leadership skills. It was the kiln that fired him into a strong, mature leader.

By contrast, a couple of months ago, I spoke with an unhappy young man who had received two promotions in a single year and was considering leaving the company because he was too bored with his progress.

The one quality that all successful business leaders have in common is tenacity. I hope that you develop yours early, doing something that isn't always fun. Leadership is the hardest and most rewarding thing you will ever do, and things that are worth doing always require perseverance.

Creating a Winning Dynamic

Here's a true story about a recent, amazing turn-around in the world of sports.

In 2012, the Boston Red Sox lost more than 90 games and finished dead last in the American League East division. It was the worst season since 1965 for this storied team, and many attributed it to the leadership failings of head coach

Bobby Valentine. Rumors abounded about staff infighting and dysfunction. Fans were deeply upset and players were unhappy. It was like a return to the bad old days of the "Curse of the Bambino," a superstition that evolved from the trading of Babe Ruth in 1918, followed by 86 years during which the Red Sox were denied a single World Series victory.

During the 2013 season, however, the Red Sox made the most spectacular turnaround in major league baseball history, winning the World Series against the St. Louis Cardinals.

How did the Red Sox go from worst to first in a single year? By making significant people changes, at all levels of the organization, which resulted in a totally different, winning culture.

First, the owners fired Valentine and brought in John Farrell, who had a completely different management style. Farrell remarked when he started that he wanted to "earn their trust, earn their respect, and create an environment in the clubhouse that is a trusting one." He made sure every team member knew what he expected, and then set out to support each of them in whatever way he could. "He was more like a father to us than a boss. He let us know from the first day of spring training that he had our backs," remarked slugger David Ortiz after the winning game.

Farrell also made some significant changes to the team lineup, acquiring Shane Victorino, Jonny Gomes, Stephen Drew, and Mike Napoli—all stellar veteran players with something to prove.

As in any winning season, other factors also contributed to the team's stunning victory, but it all started with people, as it always does.

As noted in Chapter 10, the *right* person in the *right* role is up to 300 percent more productive than an okay person.

In addition, if you succeed in placing stars in every key seat in your business, 90 percent of your HR problems will simply melt away on their own. You won't have to "manage," but you will be free to lead. This isn't an advertising slogan; it really is true.

Good luck as you hone this most-important of all leadership skills!

NOTES

Chapter 1

1. The Container Store website, *www.containerstore.com.*
2. Jim Collins, *Good to Great* (New York: Harper Business, 2001), pp. 17–62.
3. Stephen R. Covey, *The 8th Habit: From Effectiveness to Greatness,* pp. 2–3.

Chapter 3

1. See Leadership IQ website, *http://leadershipiq.com /blogs/leadershipiq/353542421-why-new-hires-fail -emotional-intelligence-vs-skills#.*

Chapter 4

1. Collins, *Good to Great,* pp. 17–62.

Chapter 5

1. Beth Axelrod, Helen Handfield-Jones, and Ed Michaels, "A New Game Plan for C Players," *Harvard Business Review,* January 2002.

Chapter 8

1. *www.generalpatton.com.*

2. Philip E. Tetlock and Dan Gardner, *Superforecasting: The Art and Science of Prediction* (Toronto: McClelland & Stewart 2015), p. 223.

3. *A Century of Innovation: The 3M Story* (Saint Paul, Minn.: 3M Company, 2002) p. 156.

Chapter 10

1. Thomas Schlosser, "If You Were a Poor Performer, You Wouldn't Be Aware of It," *Harvard Business Review,* January 2014.

2. Dr. Brad Smart, "The High Cost of Mis-Hires," *www.topgrading.com,* January 2008.

INDEX

ABOUT THE AUTHOR

Trevor Throness is a veteran coach who specializes in working with growing businesses from $2 million to $2 billion in sales. Trevor has helped hundreds of entrepreneurs, organizations, and business families fix people problems, enhance communication, attract top talent, and build exceptional cultures.

Trevor lives just outside Vancouver, Canada, with his wife, Jenn, and their four kids.

You can join Trevor's Monday morning coaching tips list by signing up at his website, *trevorthroness.com.*